Nick Vandome

iPad
for Seniors

in
easy steps

11th edition
covers all versions of iPad with iPadOS 15
(including iPad mini and iPad Pro)

In easy steps is an imprint of In Easy Steps Limited
16 Hamilton Terrace · Holly Walk · Leamington Spa
Warwickshire · United Kingdom · CV32 4LY
www.ineasysteps.com

Eleventh Edition

Notice of Liability
Every effort has been made to ensure that this book contains accurate and current information. However, In Easy Steps Limited and the author shall not be liable for any loss or damage suffered by readers as a result of any information contained herein.

Trademarks
iPad® is a registered trademark of Apple Computer, Inc. All other trademarks are acknowledged as belonging to their respective companies.

In Easy Steps Limited supports The Forest Stewardship Council (FSC), the leading international forest certification organization. All our titles that are printed on Greenpeace approved FSC certified paper carry the FSC logo.

MIX
Paper from
responsible sources
FSC® C020837

Printed and bound in the United Kingdom

ISBN 978-1-84078-944-7

Contents

1   Choosing your iPad   7

The iEverything	8
Simplicity of the iPad	9
Models and Sizes	10
Specifications Explained	11
Apple Pencil	12
Smart Keyboard	13
Before you Switch On	14
Getting Started	15
About iPadOS 15	16
Home Screen	17
Home Button	18
Opening Items	19
Using the Lock Screen	20
Charging your iPad	22

2   Around your iPad   23

iPad Settings	24
Navigating Around	26
Using the Dock	28
Widgets on the Home Screen	30
Today View Panel	35
Using the App Library	36
Using the Control Center	38
Multitasking	42
Shelf and New Windows	48
App Switcher Window	50
Keeping Notified	54
Scheduled Summary	56
Focus	58
Finding Things with Siri	62
Spotlight Search	64

3   iCloud   65

Living in the iCloud	66
Upgrading to iCloud+	68
About iCloud Drive	70
About Family Sharing	71
Using Family Sharing	72

4   Keyboard and Apple Pencil   75

It's Virtually a Keyboard	76
Moving the Keyboard	78
Entering Text	79
Editing Text	80
Keyboard Settings	82
Using Predictive Text	83
Keyboard Shortcuts	84
Using the Apple Pencil	86
Voice Typing	88

5   Knowing your Apps   89

What is an App?	90
Built-in Apps	91
About the App Store	94
Finding Apps	95
Obtaining Apps	97
Updating Apps	98
Organizing Apps	99
Deleting Apps	100

6 Keeping in Touch 101

Getting Online	102
Obtaining an Apple ID	103
Setting up an Email Account	104
Emailing	105
Text Messaging	106
Enhancing Text Messages	108
Shared with You	109
Video Chatting with FaceTime	110
Adding Social Media	115
Communication Apps	116

7 On a Web Safari 117

Around Safari	118
Safari Settings	120
Navigating Pages	121
Sidebar	122
Bookmarking Pages	123
Tab View	124
Opening New Tabs	125
Web Page Options	126

8 Staying Organized 127

Taking Notes	128
Quick Notes	132
Setting Reminders	134
Using the Calendar	136
Your iPad Address Book	138
Printing Items	139
Organization Apps	140

9 Leisure Time 141

Buying Music and More 142
Playing Music 144
Taking Photos and Videos 146
Photos Settings 147
Viewing Photos 148
Editing Photos 151
Reading Books 152
Getting the News 154
Viewing Movies and TV Shows 156
Art and Drawing 157
Cooking with your iPad 158
Staying Healthy 159
Playing Games 160

10 Traveling Companion 161

Looking Around Maps 162
Getting Directions 164
Traveling with your iPad 166
Planning your Trip 167
Viewing Flights 168
Finding Hotels 169
Converting Currency 170
Travel Apps 171

11 Practical Matters 173

Finding your iPad 174
Avoiding Viruses 176
Privacy 177
Screen Time 178
Updating Software 181
Accessibility Issues 182

Index 187

1 Choosing your iPad

It's compact, it's stylish, it's powerful; and it's perfect for anyone, of any age. This chapter introduces the iPad, its different models, the iPadOS 15 operating system and its interface, and some of the basic controls and functions, so you can quickly get up and running with this exciting tablet.

8 The iEverything

9 Simplicity of the iPad

10 Models and Sizes

11 Specifications Explained

12 Apple Pencil

13 Smart Keyboard

14 Before you Switch On

15 Getting Started

16 About iPadOS 15

17 Home Screen

18 Home Button

19 Opening Items

20 Using the Lock Screen

22 Charging your iPad

The iEverything

The iPad is a tablet computer that has gone a long way to change how we think of computers and how we interact with them. Instead of a large, static object it is effortlessly mobile, and even makes a laptop seem bulky by comparison.

But even with its compact size, the iPad still manages to pack a lot of power and functionality into its diminutive body. In this case, small is most definitely beautiful, and the range of what you can do with the iPad is considerable:

- Communicate via email, video and text messaging.

- Surf the web wirelessly.

- Add an endless number of new "apps" from the Apple App Store.

- Use a range of entertainment tools covering music, photos, video, books and games.

- Do all of your favorite productivity tasks such as word processing, creating spreadsheets or producing presentations.

- Organize your life with apps for calendars, address books, notes, reminders, and much more.

"Apps" is just a fancy name for what are more traditionally called programs in the world of computing. The iPad has several apps that come built in and ready for use. There are thousands more available to download from the online App Store (see Chapter 5).

Add to this up to 10 hours' battery life when you are on the move, a range of different sizes (with a Retina Display screen of outstanding clarity) and a seamless backup system, and it is clear why the iPad can stylishly fulfill all of your computing needs.

The New icon pictured above indicates a new or enhanced feature introduced with iPads using iPadOS 15.

Simplicity of the iPad

Computers have become a central part of our everyday lives, but there is no reason why they need to be complex devices that have us scratching our heads as to how to best use them. The iPad is not only stylish and compact; it also makes the computing process as simple as possible, so you can concentrate on what you want to do. Some ways in which this is done are:

- **Quickly on**. With the iPad there is no long wait for it to turn on, or wake from a state of sleep. When you turn it on, it is ready to use; it's as simple as that.

- **Apps**. iPad apps sit on the Home screen, visible and ready to use. Most apps are created in a similar format, so once you have mastered getting around them you will be comfortable using the majority of them.

- **Settings**. One of the built-in iPad apps is Settings. This is a one-stop shop for customizing the way that your iPad looks and operates, and also how settings for apps work.

- **Dock and App Switcher window**. These are two functions that enable you to access your favorite apps quickly, regardless of what you are doing on your iPad.

- **Home button**. This enables you to return to the main Home screen at any time. It also has some additional functionality, depending on how many times you click it.

Much of the way you navigate around the iPad is done by tapping or swiping with your fingers, rather than with a traditional keyboard and mouse. There is also a virtual keyboard for input functions.

The Dock is the bar at the bottom of the iPad screen, onto which apps can be placed for quick access.

Models and Sizes

Since its introduction in 2010, the iPad has evolved in both its size and specifications. It is now a family of devices, rather than a single size. When choosing your iPad, the first consideration is which size to select. There are four options:

Don't forget

Another variation in the iPad family is how they connect to the internet and online services. This is either with just Wi-Fi connectivity or Wi-Fi and 5G/4G connectivity (where available, but it also covers 3G). This should be considered if you need to connect to the internet with a cellular connection when you are traveling away from home. 5G, 4G and 3G enable you to connect to a mobile network to access the internet, in the same way as with a cell/mobile phone. This requires a contract with a provider of this type of service.

- **iPad**. This is the original version of the iPad, and retains the standard iPad title. Its high-resolution Retina Display screen measures 10.2 inches (diagonal). At the time of printing, the latest version is the 9th generation of the standard-size iPads and supports using the Apple Pencil and the Smart Keyboard (bought separately – see pages 12-13 for more details). The Smart Keyboard has a Smart Connector to attach it, and this ensures it works as soon as it is attached. The Apple Pencil has to be "paired" with the iPad, which involves opening **Settings > Bluetooth** and turning Bluetooth **On**. Then, attach the Apple Pencil via the Lightning Connector. It should then be paired and ready for use.

- **iPad Air**. This is similar to the standard iPad, but with a 10.5-inch display. However, it is the thinnest of the iPad models, at 6.1 mm, and supports use of the Apple Pencil and the Smart Keyboard.

- **iPad mini**. The iPad mini is similar in most respects to the larger version, except for its size. The screen is 8.3 inches (diagonal) and it weighs slightly less than the iPad and iPad Air. The iPad mini has a Liquid Retina Display screen. The latest version, at the time of printing, is the 6th-generation iPad mini, and it supports use of the Apple Pencil.

- **iPad Pro**. This is a powerful all-round iPad. It comes with either an 11- or a 12.9-inch screen. It can be used with the Apple Pencil and the Smart Keyboard and is ideal for productivity tasks.

Specifications Explained

Most models of iPad have the same range of specifications (the main difference being the screen sizes). Some of the specifications to consider are:

- **Processor**: This determines the speed at which the iPad operates and how quickly tasks are performed.

- **Storage**: This determines how much content can be stored on the iPad. Across the iPad family, the range is 64 gigabytes (GB), 128GB, 256GB, 512GB, 1 terabyte (TB) or 2TB.

- **Connectivity**: The options for this are Wi-Fi and 5G/4G/3G connectivity for the internet, and Bluetooth for connecting to other devices over short distances.

- **Cameras**: The front-facing camera is a FaceTime one, which is best for video calls or "selfies" (self-portraits). The back-facing camera is a high-resolution one that takes excellent photos and videos.

- **Screen**: iPads that can run iPadOS 15 all have Retina Display screens for the highest resolution and best clarity. This is an LED-backlit screen.

- **Operating system**: The latest version of the iPad operating system is iPadOS 15.

- **Battery power**: This is the length of time the iPad can be used for general use, such as surfing the web on Wi-Fi, watching video, or listening to music. All models offer approximately 10 hours of use in this way.

- **Input/Output**: These include a Lightning Connector port (for charging), 3.5 mm stereo headphone minijack, built-in speaker, microphone and nano-SIM card tray (Wi-Fi and 5G/4G/3G model only).

- **Sensors**: These are used to determine the amount of ambient light and also the orientation in which the iPad is being held. The sensors include an accelerometer, ambient light sensor, barometer and gyroscope.

The amount of storage you need may change once you have bought your iPad. If possible, buy a version with as much as possible, as you cannot add more later.

Some iPad models have a USB-C Connector, rather than a Lightning Connector. These include: iPad Pro 11-inch (2nd generation and later); iPad Pro 12.9-inch (3rd generation and later); iPad Air (4th generation and later); and iPad mini (6th generation and later). This is used for charging the iPad and it can also be used to connect a USB-C flashdrive and external devices using USB-C.

Apple Pencil

The Apple Pencil is a stylus that can be used on the screen instead of your finger to perform a variety of tasks. At the time of printing, it can be used with all of the iPad models. It can be used for the following:

- Drawing intricate (or simple) artwork using drawing or painting apps.

- Moving around web pages by swiping or tapping on links to access other web pages.

- Selecting items of text by tapping on them and also dragging the selection handles.

- Annotating PDF documents.

Charging the Apple Pencil

The Apple Pencil can be charged using the iPad Lightning Connector port (the same one as for charging the iPad) or the iPad's charging cable, using the Apple Pencil's Lightning adapter, which is supplied with the Apple Pencil.

To check the level of Apple Pencil charge, swipe from left to right on the Home screen to access the Today View panel (see page 35) and swipe down to the **Batteries** section (and also view the level of charge for the iPad).

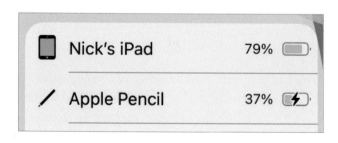

Hot tip

The Apple Pencil can be used to annotate PDF documents or screenshots simply by writing on them. This is known as Instant Markup. To annotate a screenshot, press and hold the **On/Off** button and **Home** button simultaneously to capture the screenshot. A thumbnail of the screenshot appears in the bottom left-hand corner for a few seconds. Tap once on this to expand it, and use the drawing tools at the bottom of the screen to annotate it. The annotated image can then be saved into the Photos app.

Smart Keyboard

Although the virtual keyboard on the iPad (see Chapter 4 for details) is excellent for text and data inputting or shorter pieces of writing, it is not ideal for longer tasks such as writing a vacation journal or a family history. To overcome this, the Apple Smart Keyboard has been introduced and can be used on all iPad models except the iPad mini. It is a fully-functioning external keyboard that also doubles as a cover. The Smart Keyboard is connected with the Smart Connector that matches the one on the body of the iPad.

If a Smart Keyboard is not used, the virtual one will be available instead.

Smart Keyboard Shortcuts bar

When typing with the Smart Keyboard, the same Shortcuts bar is available as with the virtual keyboard, specific to the current app.

Tap on an item on the Shortcuts bar to access it.

The Smart Keyboard also supports standard keyboard shortcuts such as:

Command + **C**: Copy.

Command + **V**: Paste.

Command + **X**: Cut.

Command + **Z**: Undo.

Command + **B**: Adds bold to selected text.

Command + **I**: Adds italics to selected text.

Command + **U**: Adds underline to selected text.

Smart Keyboard shortcuts

Some of the keyboard shortcuts that can be performed on the Smart Keyboard are:

- **Command (cmd)** + **H** – Return to Home screen.

- **Command** + **Tab** – Access the App Switcher bar, in the middle of the screen. Press the Tab button to move through the apps in the App Switcher. Stop at the app you want to open.

- **Command** + **spacebar** – Access the Spotlight Search.

- **Press and hold Command** – A list of Smart Keyboard shortcuts in specific apps.

- **Globe key** – Access available keyboards, including the emoji keyboard for adding emoji icons to text.

Don't forget

To turn on the iPad, press and hold the **On/Off** button for a few seconds. It can also be used to Sleep the iPad or Wake it from the Sleep state, by pressing it once.

Hot tip

The latest version of the iPad Air (4th generation) uses the top button on the body of the iPad to perform the functions of the Home button.

Hot tip

If your iPad ever freezes, or if something is not working properly, it can be rebooted by holding down the **Home** button and the **On/Off** button for 10 seconds and then turning it on again by pressing and holding the **On/Off** button.

Before you Switch On

The external controls for the iPad are simple. Three of them are situated at the top of the iPad and the other is in the middle, at the bottom. There are also two cameras, one on the front and one on the back of the iPad.

Controls

The controls at the top of the iPad are:

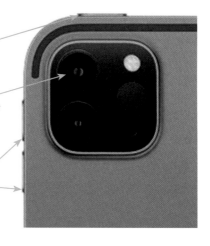

On/Off button.

Cameras. One is located on the back, underneath the On/Off button and one on the front, at the top.

Volume Up and **Down** buttons.

Home button. Press this once to wake up the iPad or return to the Home screen at any point.

Speakers. The speakers are located on the bottom edge of the iPad.

Lightning Connector. Connect the Lightning Connector here to charge the iPad, or connect it to another computer. Some iPad models have a USB-C Connector, rather than a Lightning Connector. These include: iPad Pro 11-inch (2nd generation and later); iPad Pro 12.9-inch (3rd generation and later); iPad Air (4th generation and later); and iPad mini (6th generation and later).

Getting Started

To start using the iPad, hold down the On/Off button for a few seconds. Initially, there will be a series of setup screens, some of which depend on how you set up your iPad. These settings and screens include:

- **Language** and **Country**. Select a language and country.

- **Quick Start**. This can be used to transfer settings from another compatible iOS device, such as an iPhone.

- **Written and Spoken Languages**. Select languages for keyboards and dictation.

- **Wi-Fi network**. Connect to the internet, using either your own home network or a public Wi-Fi hotspot.

- **Data & Privacy**. This is used to identify features that ask for your personal information.

- **Touch ID**. Use this on compatible models to create a Touch ID for unlocking your iPad with a fingerprint.

- **Create a Passcode**. This can be used to create a numerical passcode for unlocking your iPad.

- **Apps & Data**. This can be used to set up an iPad from an iCloud backup, or as a new iPad.

- **Apple ID and iCloud**. This can be used to use an existing iCloud account or create a new one.

- **Make this your new iPad**. If you are setting up from an iCloud backup, this can be used to specify that the iPad being set up is a new one.

- **Keep your iPad Up to Date**. This can be used to install updates to the operating system (iPadOS) automatically.

- **Improve Siri & Dictation**. This is used to set up Siri, the digital voice assistant and dictation options.

- **iPad Analytics**. This can allow details from the iPad and its apps to be sent to Apple and developers.

A lot of the initial settings can be skipped during the setup process and accessed later from the **Settings** app.

For details about obtaining an Apple ID, see page 103.

For more information about using iCloud, see pages 66-70.

iPadOS 15 is the latest operating system for the iPad.

iPadOS 15 is not compatible with some older models of iPad but can be run on: iPad mini 4 and later; iPad 5th generation and later; iPad Air 2 and later; and all models of iPad Pro. The iPad model number is on the back of the iPad – visit **https://support.apple. com/en-us/HT201471** to find out which model you have.

To check the version of iPadOS, look in **Settings** > **General** > **Software Update**.

About iPadOS 15

iPadOS 15 is the third version of the iPad operating system that is a separate version to the one used on iPhones – iOS. However, although iPadOS 15 has its own designation, it is still very closely aligned to the latest version of iOS (iOS 15). Where iPadOS 15 differs from iOS is in the iPad-specific features, such as enhanced multitasking options and Home screen widgets. Some of the new features in iPadOS 15 include:

- **Home screen widgets**. The iPad Home screen now includes a range of customizable widgets that can be used to display your most frequently accessed items.

- **Multitasking**. The multitasking options on the iPad have been expanded and simplified with iPadOS 15, including multitasking buttons on every screen that are used to access the multitasking options.

- **App Library**. The App Library is included for the first time, after it was first introduced on the iPhone. This provides access to all of the apps on the iPad.

- **Quick Notes**. The Notes app now includes a Quick Notes option, where notes can be created from any screen and then saved in the Notes app.

- **FaceTime**. FaceTime has been given an extensive overhaul and now includes options for sharing movies and music with other people on a FaceTime call, and also for sharing your screen on a call.

- **Focus**. The Focus option can be used to set conditions to limit the number of notifications you receive when you are performing specific tasks.

- **iCloud+**. The online storage facility, iCloud, has been updated with iCloud+, to give even more options.

- **Enhanced apps**. iPadOS 15 has enhanced versions of Safari, Messages and Maps.

Home Screen

Once you have completed the setup process, you will see the Home screen of the iPad. This contains the built-in apps and the Home screen widgets (at the top of the screen).

Home screen widgets is a new feature in iPadOS 15.

There are 34 different default wallpaper backgrounds for iPadOS 15 on the iPad. These can be found in **Settings** > **Wallpaper**. The options are: **Dynamic**, which means that they appear to move independently from the app icons when you tilt the iPad; and **Stills**, which are static images; and you can also use your own pictures from the Photos app.

At the bottom of the screen are seven apps that appear by default in the Dock area (left-hand side) and recently-accessed apps (right-hand side).

Rotate the iPad, and the orientation changes automatically.

Items on the Dock can be removed and new ones can be added. For more details, see pages 28-29.

Home Button

The Home button, located at the bottom middle of the iPad, can be used to perform a number of tasks:

The latest version of the iPad Air (4th generation) uses the top button on the body of the iPad to perform the functions of the Home button.

1 Click once on the **Home** button to return to the Home screen at any point

2 Double-click on the **Home** button to access the **App Switcher** window. This shows the most recently-used and open apps

For more details about the App Switcher, see pages 50-53.

Pinch together with thumb and four fingers on the screen to return to the Home screen from any open app.

3 Press and hold on the **Home** button to access Siri, the voice assistant function

For more information about using the iPad search facilities, see pages 62-64.

Opening Items

All apps on your iPad can be opened with minimal fuss and effort:

① Tap once on an icon to open the app

② The app opens at its own Home screen

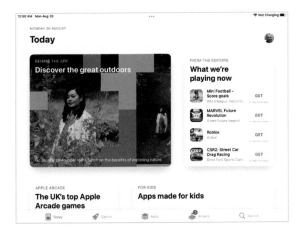

③ Click once on the **Home** button to return to the main iPad Home screen

For details about using the App Switcher, and closing items, see pages 50-53.

④ From the App Switcher window, swipe between apps and tap on one to open it directly

Don't forget

The screen can also be locked by pressing once on the **On/Off** button.

Hot tip

Notifications can be displayed on the iPad's Lock screen. This can be activated by going to **Settings** > **Notifications** > **Show Previews** and then selecting **Always**.

Don't forget

Once the passcode has been set, tap on the **Require Passcode** button in the Touch ID & Passcode section to specify when the passcode is activated. The best option is **Immediately**, otherwise someone else could access your iPad before the passcode is activated.

Using the Lock Screen

To save power, it is possible to set your iPad screen to lock automatically. This is the equivalent of the Sleep option on a traditional computer. To do this:

1 Tap once on the **Settings** app

Settings

2 Tap once on the **Display & Brightness** tab

AA Display & Brightness

3 Tap once on the **Auto-Lock** option

Auto-Lock   5 minutes >

4 Select a length of time until the iPad is locked automatically, when it is not being used

‹ Back	Auto-Lock	
2 minutes		
5 minutes		
10 minutes		✓
15 minutes		
Never		

Locking and unlocking an iPad

When the iPad is locked – i.e. the Lock screen is displayed – it can be unlocked simply by pressing the **Home** button. However, this is not secure, as anyone could unlock the iPad. A better option is to add a numerical passcode. To do this:

1 Select **Settings** > **Touch ID & Passcode**

2 Tap once on the **Turn Passcode On** button

3 Enter a 6-digit passcode. This can be used to unlock your iPad from the Lock screen. Confirm the passcode on the next screen. The passcode is now required on the Lock screen whenever the iPad is locked

Fingerprint sensor with Touch ID

For greater security, the Home button can be used as a fingerprint sensor to unlock your iPad with the unique fingerprint that has set it up. (A passcode also has to be set up in case the Touch ID does not work.) To do this:

1 Select **Settings** > **Touch ID & Passcode**

2 Create a passcode as shown on the previous page (this is required if the fingerprint sensor is unavailable for any reason).
Drag the **iPad Unlock** button **On**

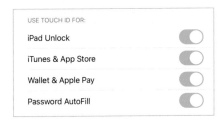

The fingerprint sensor is very effective, although it may take a bit of practice until you can get the right position for your finger to unlock the iPad first time, every time. It can only be unlocked with the same finger that created the Touch ID in Step 4. Additional fingerprints can also be set up. The Touch ID may not work if your finger is wet.

3 Tap once on the **Add a Fingerprint...** link. This presents a screen for creating your Touch ID

FINGERPRINTS

Add a Fingerprint...

4 Place your finger on the **Home** button several times to create a Touch ID. This will include capturing the edges of your finger. The screens move automatically after each part

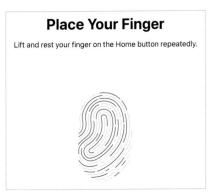

Place Your Finger

Lift and rest your finger on the Home button repeatedly.

is captured, and the fingerprint icon turns red. Complete the Touch ID wizard to create a unique fingerprint for unlocking your iPad

A "wizard" is a computer program that guides you through a process.

Charging your iPad

The iPad comes with a Lightning Connector to USB cable and a USB power adapter, for charging the iPad:

Don't forget

iPads that can run iPadOS 15 have Lightning Connectors or the newer USB-C Connector.

1 Connect the USB end of the Lightning Connector to the power adapter

2 Connect the other end of the Lightning Connector to the iPad

Hot tip

If you have older accessories with Dock connector points, you can buy a Lightning to 30-pin adapter so that you can still use them with a 4th-generation (and later) iPad.

3 Plug in the power adapter

The iPad can also be charged by connecting it with the Lightning Connector to another computer.

2 Around your iPad

Once you have turned on your iPad you will want to start using it as soon as possible. This chapter shows how to do this, with details about: settings; navigation; using the new widgets on the Home screen; accessing the Control Center; multitasking; using notifications; and searching for items with Siri and Spotlight.

24   iPad Settings

26   Navigating Around

28   Using the Dock

30   Widgets on the Home Screen

35   Today View Panel

36   Using the App Library

38   Using the Control Center

42   Multitasking

48   Shelf and New Windows

50   App Switcher Window

54   Keeping Notified

56   Scheduled Summary

58   Focus

62   Finding Things with Siri

64   Spotlight Search

Don't forget

If a Settings option has an **On/Off** button next to it, this can be changed by swiping the button to either the left or right. Green indicates that the option is **On**.

Hot tip

The Display & Brightness setting has an option for Dark Mode, which inverts the screen, with a dark background and white text. This can make the screen easier to read in certain conditions. To use Dark Mode, tap **On** the **Dark** button. To specify when Dark Mode is activated drag the **Automatic** button **On**, or tap once on the **Options** button to specify a time for Dark Mode.

iPad Settings

The Settings app controls settings for the appearance of the iPad and the way it and its apps operate:

Settings

- **Apple ID, iCloud, Media & Purchases**. This contains settings for items that are to be saved to the online iCloud service (see pages 66-70).

- **Airplane Mode**. This can be used while on an airplane.

- **Wi-Fi**. This enables you to select a wireless network.

- **Bluetooth**. Turn this **On** to connect Bluetooth devices.

- **Notifications**. This determines how the Notification Center operates (see pages 54-55).

- **Sounds**. This has options for setting sounds for alerts.

- **Focus**. Use this to specify times when you do not want to receive audio alerts or FaceTime video calls.

- **Screen Time**. This is used to view details of your iPad use and add restrictions (see pages 178-180).

- **General**. This contains a number of options for how the iPad operates. This is one of the most useful settings.

- **Control Center**. This determines how the Control Center operates (see pages 38-41).

- **Display & Brightness**. This can be used to set the screen brightness, text size and bold text.

- **Home Screen & Dock**. This has an option for the size of the Home screen icons and also displaying the Today View panel on the Home screen.

- **Accessibility**. This can be used for users with visual or motor issues (see pages 182-186 for details).

- **Wallpaper**. To change the iPad's wallpaper, tap once on the **Choose a New Wallpaper** option.

- **Siri & Search**. Options for turning on the digital voice assistant, and settings such as language and voice style.

- **Apple Pencil**. This has options for using an Apple Pencil with an iPad.

- **Touch ID & Passcode**. This has options for creating a unique fingerprint ID for unlocking your iPad (see page 21).

- **Battery**. This shows the battery usage of specific apps and can show the battery level in the status bar.

- **Privacy**. This can be used to activate Location Services so that your location can be used by specific apps.

- **App Store**. This can be used to specify download options for the App Store.

- **Wallet & Apple Pay**. This can be used to set up Apple Pay for online payments.

- **Passwords**. This contains options for managing website passwords.

- **Mail, Contacts, Calendars**. These are three separate settings, with options for how these three apps operate.

If you have an iPad with 5G/4G/3G connectivity, there will also be a setting for Cellular/Mobile.

Tap this arrow to see additional options:

iPad app settings

Most of the built-in iPad apps have their own settings that determine how the apps operate. These include: Notes, Reminders, Voice Memos, Messages, FaceTime, Safari, News, Stocks, Translate, Maps, Measure, Shortcuts, Home, Music, TV, Photos, Camera, Books, and Podcasts. Tap on one of these tabs to view the settings for that app. (Apps that are downloaded from the App Store also have their individual settings in this location in the Settings app.)

Tap once here to move back to the previous page for the selected setting:

Navigating Around

Much of the navigation on the iPad is done with Multitasking Gestures, which are combinations of tapping, swiping and pinching gestures that can be used to view items such as web pages, photos, maps and documents.

Swiping between screens

Once you have added more apps to your iPad, they will start to fill up more screens. To move between these, swipe left or right with one or two fingers.

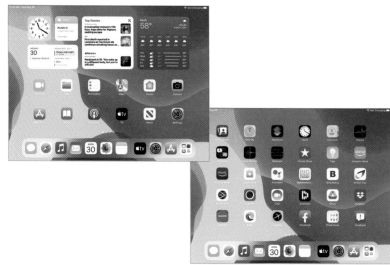

Returning to the Home screen

Pinch together with thumb and four fingers to return to the Home screen from any open app, or swipe up from the bottom of the screen. The Home screen can also be accessed by using a long swipe up from the bottom of any screen (a short swipe brings up the Dock, and a slightly longer one brings up the App Switcher).

Swiping up and down

Swipe up and down with one finger to move up or down web pages, photos, maps or documents. The content moves in the opposite direction of the swipe; i.e. if you swipe up, the page will move down, and vice versa.

Don't forget

You can also move between different screens by tapping once on one of the small white dots in the middle of the screen above the Dock, illustrated on page 28.

Don't forget

You can also return to the Home screen by clicking once on the **Home** button.

Hot tip

The faster you swipe on the screen, the faster the screen moves up or down.

Tapping and zooming
Double-tap with one finger to zoom in on a web page, photo, map or document. Double-tap with one finger to return to the original view.

Pinching and swiping
Swipe outward with thumb and forefinger to zoom in on a web page, photo, map or document.

Pinch together with thumb and forefinger to zoom back out on a web page, photo, map or document.

Swiping outward with thumb and forefinger enables you to zoom in on an item to a greater degree than double-tapping with one finger.

More Gestures
- Swipe left or right with four or five fingers to move between open apps.

- Drag with two or three fingers to move a web page, photo, map or document.

- Press and swipe down on any free area on the Home screen to access the Spotlight Search box.

- Swipe left or right with one finger to move between full-size photos in the Photos app.

- Tap once on a photo thumbnail with one finger to enlarge it to full screen within the Photos app.

- Drag down from the top right-hand corner of any screen to access the Control Center.

- Drag down at the top middle of the iPad to view current notifications in the Notification Center.

Using the Dock

The Dock is an element that has been part of the iPad since it was introduced. The Dock has two separate sections: the standard Dock area for your most frequently-used apps, and a section for recently-used apps, those open on another Apple device, and the App Library icon.

Elements of the Dock

Standard apps (by default, these are Messages, Safari, Music, Mail, Calendar, Photos and Notes) are displayed on the left-hand side of the Dock.

Hot tip

Just above the Dock is a line of small dots. These indicate how many Home screens of content there are on the iPad. Tap on one of the dots to go to that Home screen, or swipe to the left or right to move between them. The white dot indicates the position of the current Home screen being viewed.

Dynamic items that change each time a new app is opened, or certain apps opened on another Apple device using iPadOS, iOS or macOS are displayed on the right-hand side (and also the App Library icon at the far right-hand side).

Don't forget

The functionality of open apps on other Apple devices is known as **Handoff** and can be turned On or Off in **Settings** > **General** > **AirPlay & Handoff**.

If a compatible app is open on another Apple device – e.g. an iPhone – this label appears in the right-hand corner. Tap on the app to open the same item as it is displaying on the other

Apple device. Apps that operate in this way are those linked through iCloud, and include the web browser Safari, Mail, Messages, Reminders, Calendar, Contacts, and Notes. The icon on the far right-hand side of the Dock is for the App Library; see pages 36-37 for details.

Adding and removing Dock items

The default items on the Dock can be removed and other apps added, as required. To do this:

1 Press on an item on the Dock and drag it onto the main area of the Home screen

2 Repeat the process for an app on the Home screen to drag it onto the Dock

Accessing the Dock

The Dock can also be accessed from any app, not just from the Home screen. To do this:

1 From within any app, use a short swipe up from the bottom of the screen to access the Dock

Don't forget

Up to 14 apps can be added to the left-hand side of the Dock. However, this reduces the size at which the apps' icons appear. There are only ever four items on the right-hand side of the Dock, and this changes each time a new app is opened or accessed (unless it is already in the main area of the Dock).

Hot tip

Press the **Home** button once to return to the Home screen, displaying the Dock, from any app.

Widgets on the Home Screen

The iPad Home screen contains icons for the apps that can be accessed, and also widgets containing items of useful information, which are located at the top of the Home screen.

Widgets on the Home screen is a new feature in iPadOS 15.

By default, these widgets are, from left to right: the Clock widget; the Notes widget; the Calendar widget; and two stacks of widgets (several widgets together), initially displaying the News widget and the Weather widget.

Press and hold anywhere on the Home screen to access the editing controls for the widgets.

...cont'd

To use the widgets on the Home screen:

1 Tap once on an individual widget to open the full version of the app

2 For stacks, swipe up or down to view the other widgets in a stack

3 Tap once on the active widget in a stack to open the full version of the app

Beware

4 Press and hold a widget to access its own menu options

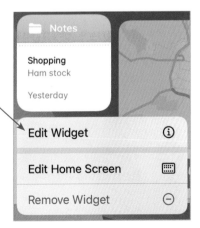

Widgets cannot be placed within another widget: if they are moved over another widget, it will move aside to accommodate the first widget.

...cont'd

Moving widgets

The widgets on the Home screen can be moved around, so you can order the panel exactly how you want. To do this:

Widgets can also be removed by accessing the widget controls and tapping once on the **–** button in the top left-hand corner. Tap once on the **Remove** button to remove the widget from the Home screen.

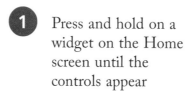

1 Press and hold on a widget on the Home screen until the controls appear

2 Drag the widget into a new position. Widgets remain at their selected sizes, and other widgets will be reordered to accommodate the moved widget accordingly

Removing Home screen widgets

The widgets on the Home screen can be removed, to give more room on the Home screen. To do this:

To remove all of the Home screen widgets, repeat the process in Step 2 for removing Home screen widgets for all of the widgets and stacks.

1 Press and hold on a widget until its menu appears. Tap once on the **Remove Widget** button

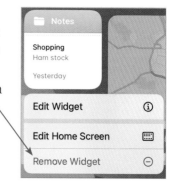

2 Tap once on the **Remove** button

Adding Home screen widgets

The widgets on the Home screen can be customized to display different apps and at different sizes. To do this:

1 Press and hold on the Home screen widgets until they start to wobble (or, if they have all been removed, press and hold anywhere on the Home screen)

2 Tap once the **+** button in the top left-hand corner

3 The Widgets Library is displayed. The main panel contains suggested widgets to use. The left-hand sidebar contains a full list of available widgets. The Search box at the top of the window can be used to search for specific widgets

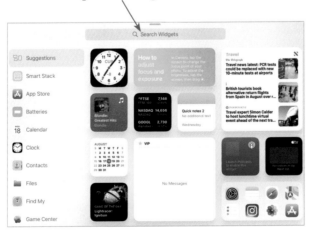

Don't forget

If all of the widgets are removed from the Home screen, the apps on the Home screen will be rearranged to take up the available space. If widgets are then reinstated, they will take up their original position on the Home screen.

33

...cont'd

4 Tap once on a widget to view options for adding it to the Home screen. Swipe from right to left, or tap on the dots toward the bottom of the window, to access the different sizes and formats at which the widget can be used

5 Tap once on the **Add Widget** button

6 The widget is added to the Home screen, at the size selected in Step 4

Editing widgets and stacks

Some of the widgets can be edited, depending on their functionality. To do this:

1 Press and hold on a widget to access its menu. Tap once on the **Edit Widget** button, if this is available

2 Apply the editing options for the widget, as required

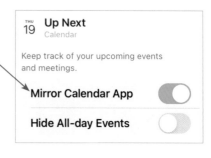

Don't forget

Stacks can also be edited from the Home screen. To do this, press and hold on the stack and tap once on the **Edit Stack** button.

Today View Panel

The Today View panel contains similar widgets to the Home screen, but they are not displayed on the Home screen. To use the Today View panel:

1 Swipe from left to right on the left-hand edge of the Home screen to access the Today View panel, which contains the Today View widgets

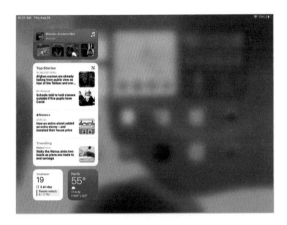

2 Press and hold anywhere within the Today View panel to access its editing controls. Tap once on the **+** button to add more widgets. Tap once on the **-** button to remove a widget

3 Swipe up on the Today View panel to see all of the widgets currently in it. Tap once on the **Edit** button at the bottom of the Today View panel to access the editing controls for the widgets, including the **Customize** option (see Hot tip)

Edit

Hot tip

Tap once on the **Customize** button, accessed from the **Edit** button in Step 3, to access options for adding widgets to the Today View.

Customize

Using the App Library

By default, apps on iPads with iPadOS have appeared on separate Home screens, once there are too many for one Home screen. While this is still the case, iPadOS 15 can also display all of the apps on the device, organized in separate categories and folders. This is known as the App Library. To use the App Library to work with and manage the apps on your iPad:

The App Library is a new feature in iPadOS 15.

1 Tap once on the App Library icon on the Dock

2 Apps in the App Library are automatically organized into appropriate folders. Tap once on an app in a folder to open it

3 Tap on the corner of a folder to open it and view all of the apps within it

4 Press and hold anywhere on the App Library page to access the control buttons. Tap once on this button to delete an app from your iPad

Viewing apps
To view all of the apps in the App Library:

1 Swipe downward anywhere within the App Library

2 All of the available apps are listed alphabetically

3 Swipe up and down to view all of the available apps, or tap on the alphabetic sidebar to move to that section

4 Use the Search box at the top of the App Library window to search for specific apps. As you type, matching apps will appear below the Search box

Using the Control Center

The Control Center is a panel containing commonly-used options within the **Settings** app, and is an excellent option for when you do not want to have to go into Settings.

Accessing the Control Center

The Control Center can be accessed from any screen within iPadOS 15, and it can also be accessed from the Lock screen.

1 Swipe down from the top right-hand corner of the Home screen, from any app, or from the Lock screen to access the Control Center panel

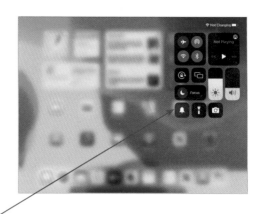

Control Center functionality

The Control Center contains items that have differing formats and functionality. To access these:

Don't forget

AirDrop is the functionality for sharing items wirelessly between compatible devices. Tap once on the **AirDrop** button in the Control Center and specify whether you want to share with **Contacts Only** or **Everyone**. Once AirDrop is set up, you can use the **Share** button in compatible apps to share items such as photos with any other AirDrop users in the vicinity.

1 Press on the folder of four icons to access the **Airplane Mode**, **AirDrop**, **Wi-Fi** and **Bluetooth** options

2 Press on the **Music** button to expand the options for music controls, including playing or pausing items and changing the volume. Tap once on this icon to send music from your iPad to other compatible devices, such as AirPod earphones or HomePods (Apple's wireless speakers)

When **Airplane Mode** is activated in the second Step 1 on the previous page, the network and wireless connectivity on the iPad is disabled. However, it can still be used for functions such as playing music or reading books, as long as they have been downloaded to the iPad.

3 Tap once on individual buttons to turn items On or Off (they change color depending on their state)

Press on the brightness and volume buttons to access panels that allow greater precision by dragging on their respective bars.

4 Drag on these items to increase or decrease the screen brightness and the volume

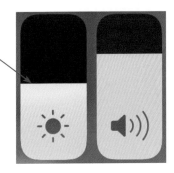

...cont'd

Don't forget

The Control Center also has a Screen Mirroring option, for displaying what is on the iPad on a compatible High-Definition TV.

Hot tip

Press on the **Flashlight** button to access bars for the strength of the flashlight. Drag on the bars to alter the level of the flashlight.

Control Center options

Items in the Control Center can be accessed as follows:

- Tap once on this button to turn **Airplane Mode** On or Off.

- Tap once on this button to activate **AirDrop** for sharing items with other AirDrop users.

- Tap once on this button to turn **Wi-Fi** On or Off.

- Tap once on this button to turn **Bluetooth** On or Off.

- Tap once on this button to **Lock** or **Unlock** screen rotation. If it is locked, the screen will not change when you change the orientation of your iPad.

- Tap once on this button to **Mute** all sounds.

- Tap once on this button to turn **Focus** mode On or Off.

- Tap once on this button to turn On the **Flashlight**. Press on the button to access the option to change the brightness (see Hot tip).

- Tap once on this button to open the **Camera** app. Press on the button to access options for taking a selfie (a self-portrait), recording a video, recording a slow-motion video, and taking a standard photo.

Customizing the Control Center

The items in the Control Center can be customized – i.e. items can be added or removed. To do this:

1 Tap once on the **Settings** app

2 Tap once on the **Control Center** tab

3 The items currently in the Control Center are shown at the top of the window; those that can be added are below them.

INCLUDED CONTROLS

⊖ 🔕 Silent Mode ≡

⊖ 🔦 Flashlight ≡

⊖ 📷 Camera ≡

MORE CONTROLS

⊕ Accessibility Shortcuts

⊕ ⏰ Alarm

⊕ Apple TV Remote

⊕ Code Scanner

Tap once on a red icon to remove an existing item, or tap once on a green icon to add new items to the Control Center

4 Items that are added in Step 3 are included in the Control Center, and can be accessed from here

Hot tip

Dark Mode, for changing the screen background and text color, can also be added to the Control Center, from the list further down the screen in Step 3.

41

Multitasking

The iPad has evolved from being an internet-enabled communication and entertainment device into something that is now a genuine productivity device. With iPadOS 15, productivity options are enhanced with a range of multitasking options including Split View, Slide Over and Main Window. Options for accessing these, and working with them, has been made easier in iPadOS 15. To use the multitasking options:

The multitasking options have been updated in iPadOS 15.

1 Open the first app that you want to use

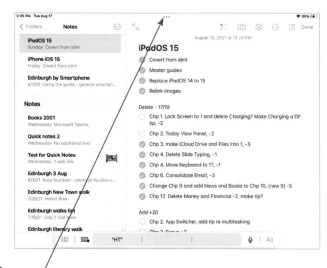

2 The buttons at the top of the app can be used to access the multitasking options. Tap once on the buttons

3 The multitasking options are, from left to right: Full Window; Split View; and Slide Over. Tap once on each option to apply it for the selected app

Using Split View

Split View enables two apps to be used side by side, independently of each other. For instance, you can look through a page on the web with Safari in one view, and then add notes in the Notes app in the other view. To use Split View for multitasking:

1 Open the first app that you want to use and tap once on the multitasking buttons at the top of the window, as shown on the previous page

2 Tap once on the **Split View** button (middle button)

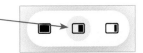

3 The app is minimized to the right-hand side of the screen and the Home screen is displayed

The multitasking buttons at the top of the screen prompt you to select another app for Split View, once the Split View button has been selected in Step 2.

4 Tap once on an app on the Home screen, or on the Dock, to activate it as the other app in Split View

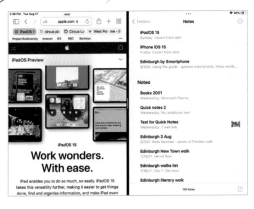

...cont'd

5 The two apps are displayed side by side. Initially, the apps in Split View take up 50% of the screen each and can be used independently of each other

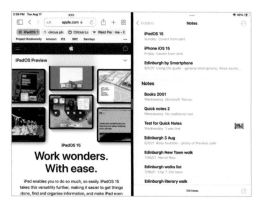

Tap once on the multitasking buttons in either of the Split View windows and tap once on the Full Window button (left-hand button) to make that window full screen, and close Split View. See page 47 for more details.

6 Drag on the middle button to change the proportions of the two Split View panels

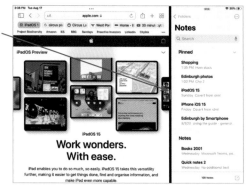

7 Press and hold on the middle button and drag it away from the right-hand (or left-hand) edge of the screen to close one of the Split View apps

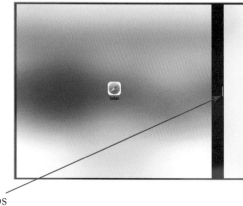

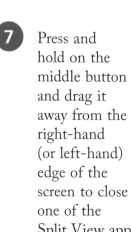

Using Slide Over view

Slide Over view is similar to Split View, except the second app appears as a floating panel over the initial one. Also, the Slide Over panel can contain multiple apps. To use Slide Over view for multitasking:

1 Open the first app that you want to use and tap once on the multitasking buttons at the top of the window, as shown on page 42

2 Tap once on the **Slide Over** view button (right-hand button)

3 The app is minimized to the right-hand side of the screen and the Home screen is displayed

4 Tap once on an app on the Home screen, or on the Dock, to activate it in Slide Over view

Don't forget

The multitasking buttons at the top of the screen prompt you to select another app for Slide Over view, once the Slide Over button has been selected in Step 2.

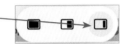

Hot tip

For the app in Slide Over view, tap once on the multitasking buttons and tap once on the Split View button (middle button) to change to this view.

...cont'd

Hot tip

Multiple apps can be added to the panel in Slide Over view, by dragging up from the bottom of the screen to display the Dock, and then dragging more apps into the Slide Over panel. Press on the dark bar at the bottom of the app and swipe to the right to reveal the next available app in Slide Over view.

5 Press and hold on the buttons at the top of the Slide Over panel to drag it to either side of the screen (or swipe on the buttons, from right to left)

6 The two apps can be used independently of each other; e.g. move through different web pages in Safari or search locations in Maps

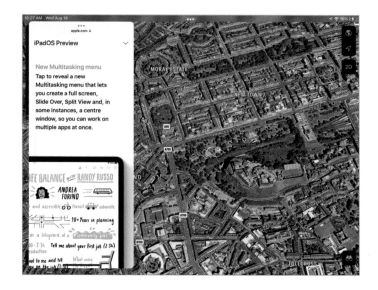

...cont'd

Using Full Window view

From either Split View or Slide Over view it is possible to return to Full Window view for any apps being used. To do this for each view:

1 In Split View, or Slide Over view, tap once on the multitasking buttons for either app

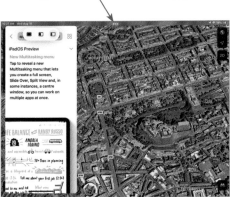

Hot tip

The options for accessing Split View and Slide Over have been simplified in iPadOS 15, with the multitasking buttons. However, they can both still be accessed in the original way. To do this, open one app and drag up from the bottom of the screen to display the Dock. Press and hold on another app and drag it to the side of the screen to create Split View, or drag it over the first app to create Slide Over.

2 Tap once on the Full Window button (left-hand button)

3 The apps are both displayed at full size

Shelf and New Windows

Another multitasking option is the Shelf, which can be thought of as a temporary storage location within compatible apps, so you can keep one item open while you are looking at something else. The apps that support this feature are Notes, Safari and Mail. The Shelf also enables new windows to be opened and used for the apps. To use the Shelf:

The Shelf is a new feature in iPadOS 15.

1 Open one of the apps that supports the Shelf – e.g. the Notes app

2 Press and hold on a note in the left-hand sidebar until its menu appears. Tap once on the **Open in New Window** button

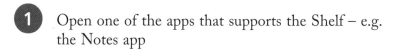

3 The note opens in its own window, floating over the main Notes window

Tap once on the **Close** button in the top left-hand corner of the window in Step 3 to close the window without adding it to the Shelf.

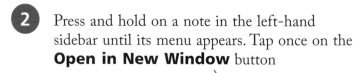

4 Tap once anywhere on the main Notes window. The note in the new window is now placed on the Shelf, displayed at the bottom of the window. Tap once on an item on the Shelf to make it the active one

5 Tap once on the multitasking button at the top of the main Notes window to access the items in the Shelf at the bottom of the screen

6 Tap once on an item on the Shelf to make it the active one. Tap once on the **New Window** button to open a new window for the app

To remove items from the Shelf, press and hold on them and swipe them to the top of the screen.

Using the Shelf in Safari
To use new windows and the Shelf in Safari:

1 Open a web page in Safari, then swipe up from the bottom of the screen to access the Dock and tap once on the Safari icon

2 The currently-open page is displayed on the Shelf. Tap once on the **New Window** button to open a new window for Safari

The Shelf can also be accessed in Notes and Mail in the same way as for Safari; i.e. open the app and then access the same app again from the Dock, to activate the Shelf and the **New Window** button.

Using the Shelf in Mail
Using the Shelf in Mail is similar to using it in Notes: press and hold on an email in your Inbox in Mail and tap on the **Open in New Window** button in the same way as in Step 2 on the previous page. Access the email in the same way as for a note on the previous page, and access the Shelf in the same way too.

App Switcher Window

The App Switcher feature in iPadOS 15 performs a number of shortcuts and useful tasks:

● It shows open apps and enables you to move between these and access them by tapping once on the required item.

● It enables apps to be closed (see next page).

Accessing App Switcher

The App Switcher window can be accessed from any screen on your iPad, as follows:

Don't forget

Press the **Home** button once to exit the App Switcher and return to the app you were using immediately before accessing the App Switcher.

Hot tip

Swipe up from the bottom of the screen slightly further than the middle of the screen to return to the Home screen, rather than the App Switcher.

1 Double-click on the **Home** button, or

2 Swipe up from the bottom of any screen. This should be a long swipe, up to the middle of the screen at least. A short swipe will bring up the Dock at the bottom of the screen, rather than the App Switcher

3 Tap on an app in the App Switcher to make it the active one

Closing apps

The iPad deals with open apps very efficiently. They rarely interact with other apps, which increases security and also means that they can be open in the background, without using up a significant amount of processing power, in a state of semi-hibernation until they are needed. Because of this, it is not essential to close apps when you move to something else. However, you may want to close apps if you feel you have too many open or if one stops working. To do this:

1 Access the App Switcher window. The currently-open apps are displayed

2 Press and hold on an app and swipe it to the top of the screen to close it. This does not remove it from the iPad and it can be opened again in the usual way

3 The app is removed from its position in the App Switcher window and the other apps move to fill the space

When you switch from one app to another, the first one stays open in the background. You can go back to it by accessing it from the App Switcher window or the Home screen.

Swipe left and right in the App Switcher window to view all of the open apps.

51

...cont'd

Creating Split View windows

Split View windows can also be created from the App Switcher, and when they are selected from here, the Split View will be displayed. Also, once a Split View window has been created in the App Switcher, if either of the included apps are selected elsewhere (e.g. from the Dock) they will appear in the Split View window. To create a Split View window in the App Switcher:

1 Access the App Switcher, as shown on page 50

2 Press and hold on one of the thumbnail images in the App Switcher

3 Drag the selected item over another thumbnail and release it

4 A Split View window is created

Don't forget

Tap once on the Split View window in the App Switcher to open the window, with the two apps available.

5 To change the items in a Split View window in the App Switcher, press and hold on another thumbnail and drag it over the item to be replaced in the Split View window. The replaced item returns as a thumbnail in the App Switcher

Numerous apps can be changed within the Split View window in Step 5, but only two can be included at any one time.

53

6 To remove items from a Split View window, press and hold on one of the Split View panels and drag it away from the Split View window, into the App Switcher window

Keeping Notified

Although the Notification Center feature is not an app in its own right, it can be used to display information from a variety of apps. The notifications appear as a list of all the items you want to be reminded about or made aware of. Notifications are set up within the Settings app. To do this:

1 Tap once on the **Settings** app

2 Tap once on the **Notifications** tab

3 In the **Notification Style** section, tap once on an item to determine how it operates when it displays a notification

Don't forget

Use the Scheduled Summary (tap once on the **Scheduled Summary** button in the main **Notifications** window) to specify settings for grouping notifications and displaying them at specific time. See pages 56-57 for details.

4 Drag the **Allow Notifications** button **On** to allow notifications to be displayed for this item

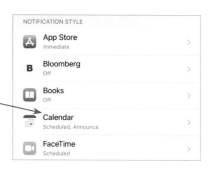

5 Make selections for how you want the notification to appear. This includes the Lock screen, the Notification Center, and as an onscreen banner

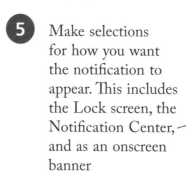

6 Drag the **Time Sensitive Notifications** button **On** to enable notifications to be displayed as soon as they become active, if they are time-specific; e.g. for a calendar event at a specific time

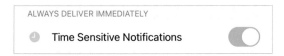

Viewing notifications

Once the Notifications settings have been selected, they can be used to keep up-to-date with all of your important appointments and reminders via the Notification Center. To view the Notification Center:

1 Drag down from the top of any screen to view the Notification Center. This displays items that have been selected, as shown on the previous page. Tap once on an item to open it in its own app

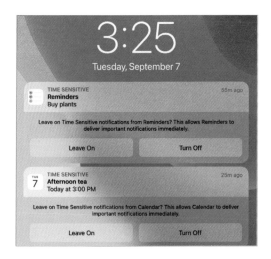

2 If the **Time Sensitive Notifications** option has been turned **On**, as in Step 6 above, there are options to **Leave On** or **Turn Off**

55

Hot tip

For each app that has had notifications turned On, there is an option to group the notifications so that they are all displayed together in the Notification Center. To do this, access the required app in the Notifications settings and tap once on the **Notifications Grouping** option and specify how these are displayed.

Scheduled Summary

As you use more and more apps on the iPad, the number of notifications can mount up too. In order to make this more manageable, certain notifications can be grouped together and displayed on a daily basis, according to a schedule that you set. To do this:

The Scheduled Summary is a new feature in iPadOS 15.

1 Tap once on the **Settings** app

2 Tap once on the **Notifications** tab

3 Tap once on the **Scheduled Summary** option

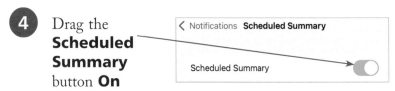

4 Drag the **Scheduled Summary** button **On**

5 Tap once on the **Continue** button

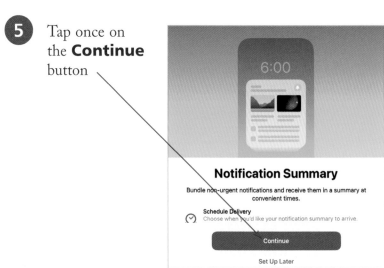

6 Select the apps to be included in the Scheduled Summary, by tapping once on the radio button next to them so that a check mark appears

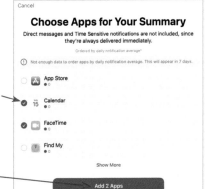

7 Tap once on the **Add Apps** button

8 Select options for how the Scheduled Summary is delivered. This includes specifying a time for the summary to appear, and adding more summaries, if required

A radio button is a round button next to an item that can be turned On or Off by tapping on it once. Multiple radio buttons can be turned On within one list of items.

9 Tap once on the **Turn on Notification Summary** button

10 Details of the Scheduled Summary are displayed in the Scheduled Summary section of the Notifications tab in the Settings app

11 A summary of the notifications specified in Step 8 is displayed at the selected time

Focus

Another option for managing your notifications is the Focus function, which can be used to control when you are notified for certain items. The Focus function can be used to limit notifications when you are performing certain actions (e.g. reading or relaxing) and it can also specify certain people and apps that are allowed to contact you and send notifications. The Focus function can be set up within the Settings app, and also accessed from the Control Center. To do this:

Focus is a new feature in iPadOS 15.

Don't forget

The Focus feature contains Do Not Disturb, which was a stand-alone feature in previous versions of iPadOS. To set this up, tap once on the **Do Not Disturb** button in Step 3 and select the required options and times for when you want Do Not Disturb to operate.

1 Tap once on the **Settings** app

2 Tap once on the **Focus** tab

3 Tap once on the **+** button in the top right-hand corner

4 The range of settings options for Focus is displayed. Tap once on one; e.g. the **Personal** button

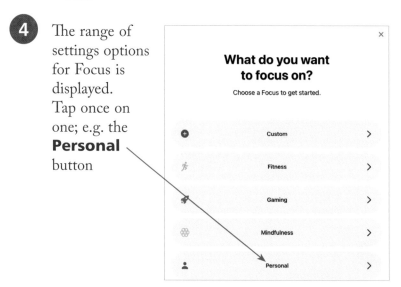

58

Don't forget

Different Focuses can be set for specific activities, and the settings for the Focus can be applied according to the required activity.

5 Tap once on the **Next** button

6 Tap once on the **Add Person** button, to add someone from whom notifications can still appear

If you add too many people in Step 6, this could negate the effect of using the specific Focus.

7 Tap once on someone from your Contacts list to select them (or select multiple people) and tap once on the **Done** button

8 The selected person is added to your **Allowed People** list

9 Tap once on the **Allow [1] Person** button

...cont'd

10 Tap once on the **Add App** button, to select apps that can still send you notifications when the Focus is on

11 Tap once on an app to select it (or select multiple apps) and tap once on the **Done** button

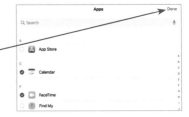

Only some of the built-in iPad apps can be added in Step 11, not any third-party ones that have been downloaded from the App Store.

12 Drag the **Time Sensitive** button **On** to enable apps that have not been selected as being allowed to still send notifications if they are time-sensitive

13 Tap once on the **Allow [2] Apps** button

14 Tap once on the **Done** button

15 Details about the
Focus are displayed
in the Focus
section of the
Settings app. Drag
the button next to
the Focus **On** to
activate it

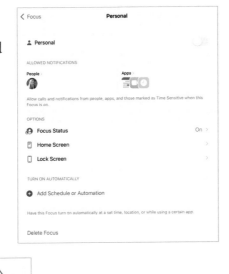

16 Details of Focuses can be
accessed from the Control
Center, by tapping on the
Focus button. Drag down
from the top right-hand
corner of any window to
access the Control Center
and tap once on this button
(if a Focus has not been set
up, the button will display
Focus)

Tap once on the menu
button on a Focus
in Step 17 to access
options for applying
how long the Focus is
activated for.

17 Details of any Focus
settings are displayed. Tap
once on a Focus to turn it
On or **Off**, or tap once on
the **New Focus** button to
create a new one

Finding Things with Siri

Siri is the iPad digital voice assistant that provides answers to a variety of questions, by looking within your iPad and also with the use of web services. You can ask Siri questions relating to the apps on your iPad, and also general questions such as weather conditions around the world, or sports results. Initially, Siri can be set up within the **Settings** app:

Hot tip

Siri can be used to open any of the built-in iPad apps, simply by saying, for example: "**Open Photos**".

1 Tap once on the **Siri & Search** option

 Siri & Search

2 Tap once on the options to select a language, set voice feedback, and allow access to your details (Siri can also be set up when you first start to use your iPad)

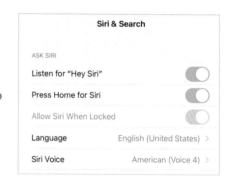

Siri & Search	
ASK SIRI	
Listen for "Hey Siri"	
Press Home for Siri	
Allow Siri When Locked	
Language	English (United States) >
Siri Voice	American (Voice 4) >

Questioning Siri

Once you have set up Siri, you can start putting it to work with your queries. To do this:

Hot tip

Turn **On** the **Listen for "Hey Siri"** button in the first Step 2 to activate Siri just by saying this phrase, without having to press the **Home** button.

1 Hold down the **Home** button until the Siri window appears

2 To find something within your iPad apps, make a request such as **Show me my calendar**

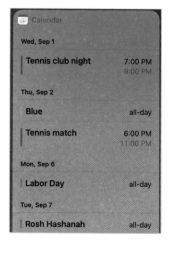

Calendar	
Wed, Sep 1	
Tennis club night	7:00 PM 9:00 PM
Thu, Sep 2	
Blue	all-day
Tennis match	6:00 PM 11:00 PM
Mon, Sep 6	
Labor Day	all-day
Tue, Sep 7	
Rosh Hashanah	all-day

Siri can also find information from across the web and related web services:

1 Siri can provide sports results for certain sports in certain countries, such as in response to the request **Show Red Sox latest score**

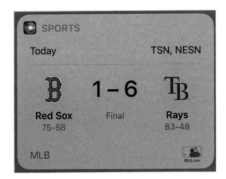

2 Global weather reports are another of Siri's strong points, and it can provide forecasts in response to the request **Show me the hourly weather in Athens**

3 Siri can also display a range of information in relation to nearby establishments such as restaurants, movie theaters and museums. Try asking, **Show me nearby Mexican restaurants**

Don't forget

Siri can be used with a range of Apple and specific third-party apps. For instance, you can ask it to find specific photos in the Photos app, send a message to someone with the Messages app, and even book restaurants and taxis with compatible apps.

Spotlight Search

Items can also be searched for using the Spotlight Search option. To do this:

1 Swipe downward on the Home screen to access the **Spotlight** Search box

Hot tip

Spotlight Search can also be used to search for local businesses and services, such as local restaurants and movie theaters, either by using specific names or by asking it to show a certain type of restaurant nearby.

2 Enter a keyword or phrase in the Search box at the top of the window

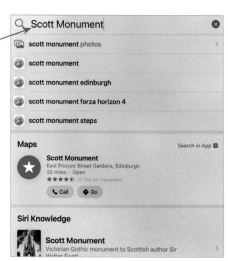

3 Swipe up the panel to view all of the search results

3 iCloud

This chapter shows how to use the online iCloud services for storing and sharing content.

66 Living in the iCloud

68 Upgrading to iCloud+

70 About iCloud Drive

71 About Family Sharing

72 Using Family Sharing

Living in the iCloud

iCloud is the Apple online service that performs a number of valuable functions:

- It makes your content available across multiple devices. The content is stored in iCloud and then pushed out to other iCloud-enabled devices, including the iPhone, iPod Touch, and other Mac or Windows computers.

- It enables online access to your content via the iCloud website. This includes your iCloud email, Contacts, Calendar, Notes, and Reminders.

- It can back up the content of your iPad.

Once you have registered for and set up iCloud, it works automatically so you do not have to worry about anything. You can activate iCloud when you first set up your iPad, or:

Hot tip

To access your iCloud account through the website, access www.icloud.com and enter your Apple ID details (see page 103).

1 Tap once on the **Settings** app

2 At the top of the Settings panel, tap once on the **Sign in to your iPad** option

3 If you already have an Apple ID, enter your details and tap once on the **Next** button

4 If you do not yet have an Apple ID, tap once on the **Don't have an Apple ID or forgot it?** link and follow the steps to create your Apple ID

...cont'd

iCloud settings

After you have set up your iCloud account you can then apply settings for how it works. Once you have done this, you will not have to worry about it again:

1 Tap once on the **Apple ID, iCloud, Media & Purchases** tab of the Settings app

2 Tap once on the **iCloud** button

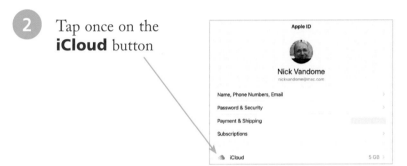

3 Drag these buttons **On** for items you want to be synced with iCloud. Each item is then saved and stored in iCloud, and made available to other iCloud-enabled devices

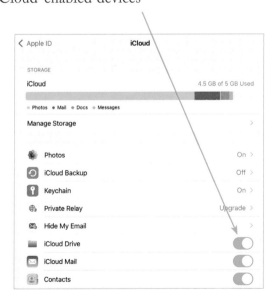

Tap once on the **Photos** option to access settings for storing and using your photos in iCloud.

Another useful iCloud function is iCloud Keychain (**Settings** > **Apple ID** > **iCloud** > **Keychain**). If this is enabled, it can keep all of your passwords and credit card information up-to-date across multiple devices and remember them when you use them on websites. The information is encrypted and controlled through your Apple ID.

Upgrading to iCloud+

iCloud+ is an enhancement to iCloud that enables you to add more storage to your iCloud account, and also access new security options. To subscribe to iCloud+:

iCloud+ is a new feature in iPadOS 15.

Don't forget

iCloud+ is the equivalent of the iCloud upgrade service, from the free version, in previous versions of iPadOS. iCloud+ also has a few additional features – see the next page for details.

Don't forget

Prices are shown in local currencies.

1 Tap once on the **iCloud** button as shown in Step 2 on page 67

2 The amount of storage that has been used is indicated by the colored bar at the top of the window (e.g. yellow for photos, and blue for email). Tap once on the **Manage Storage** option

3 Tap once on the **Upgrade** button to increase the amount of storage (the default amount is 5GB, which is provided free of charge), using the iCloud+ service

4 Select an iCloud+ storage plan

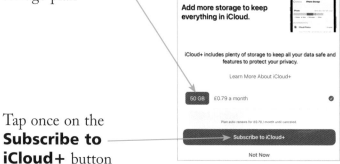

5 Tap once on the **Subscribe to iCloud+** button

6 Details of the iCloud+ options are displayed. Tap once on each option to view information about them. Tap once on the **Done** button

Private Relay and Hide My Email are new features in iPadOS 15.

7 The iCloud storage is increased, according to the new iCloud+ storage plan

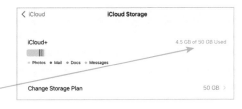

8 Tap once on the **iCloud** button in Step 7 to return to the main iCloud page

9 Tap once the **Private Relay** and **Hide My Email** options to use these for internet and email security options

10 For **Private Relay** drag the **Private Relay** button **On** to protect your browsing activity with Safari

Private Relay protects your browsing by ensuring that any website interactions are encrypted from your iPad, and two separate internet relays are used to hide your IP address linked to your iPad.

11 For **Hide My Email** tap once on the **Create New Address** button to create a random email address that is used to forward messages to your own email account, so that people cannot see your email address

+ Create New Address

About iCloud Drive

One of the options in the iCloud section is for iCloud Drive. This can be used to store documents so that you can use them on any other Apple devices that you have, such as an iPhone or a MacBook. With iCloud Drive (and the Files app) you can start work on a document on one device and continue on another device from where you left off.

Beware

If using iCloud Drive-compatible apps (such as **Pages**, **Numbers** and **Keynote**), they should be updated to their latest versions via the App Store (see page 98).

Hot tip

Tap once on the **Files** app on the Home screen to view items that have been saved in iCloud Drive.

1 Tap once on the **Apple ID, iCloud, Media & Purchases** tab of the Settings app

2 Tap once on the **iCloud** button

3 By default, iCloud Drive is set to **Off**

4 Slide the **iCloud Drive** button to green to turn it **On**

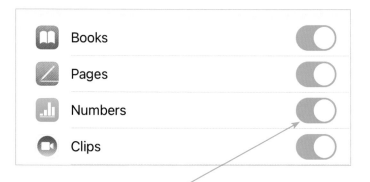

5 Drag the buttons **On** for the apps that you want to activate for syncing files with iCloud Drive. Content that you create with these apps will be stored in iCloud Drive and be available within the same apps on other devices

About Family Sharing

In iPadOS 15, the Family Sharing function enables you to share items that you have downloaded from the App Store, such as music and movies, with up to six other family members, as long as they have an Apple ID account. Once this has been set up, it is also possible to share items such as family calendars and photos, and even see where family members are on a map. To set up Family Sharing:

1 Access the **iCloud** section within the Settings app, as shown on page 67

2 Tap once on the **Family Sharing** button

3 Tap once on the **Set Up Your Family** button

4 Tap once on the **Invite People** button to invite family members or friends to join your Family Sharing. This includes music, storage plans, iTunes and App Store purchases, and location sharing for finding a lost or stolen Apple device

5 Complete the setup process by confirming your iCloud account, and specify a payment method for items that are purchased through Family Sharing

Hot tip

If children are using Family Sharing you can specify that they have to ask permission before downloading content from the iTunes Store, the App Store or the Books Store. To do this, select them in the **Family Sharing** section of the **iCloud** settings and drag the **Ask To Buy** button **On**. For each purchase you will be sent a notification asking for approval.

Using Family Sharing

Once you have set up Family Sharing and added family members, you can start sharing a selection of items.

Sharing photos

Photos can be shared with Family Sharing thanks to the Family album that is created automatically within the Photos app. To use this:

1. Tap once on the **Photos** app

2. Tap once on this button to access the sidebar

3. The **Family** album is already available in the **Shared Albums** section. Tap once on the album to open it

4. Tap once on this button to add photos to the album

5. Tap on the photos you want to add, and tap once on the **Done** button

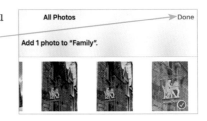

6. Make sure the **Family** album is selected as the Shared Album, and tap once on the **Post** button

Beware

Shared Albums has to be turned **On** to enable sharing photos with other family members (**Settings > Photos > Shared Albums**).

Hot tip

When someone else in your Family Sharing circle adds a photo to the Family album, you are notified in the Notification Center and also by a red notification badge on the Photos app.

Sharing calendars

Family Sharing also generates a Family calendar that can be used by all Family Sharing members:

1 Tap once on the **Calendar** app

2 Create a calendar event (as shown on pages 136-137), tap on the **Calendar** button and select the Family calendar to add the event to a calendar that all members of Family Sharing can see

All-day	⬤
Starts	May 1, 2022
Ends	May 1, 2022
Repeat	Never >
Calendar	• Family >

Hot tip

To change the color tag for a calendar, tap once on the **Calendars** button in the top left-hand corner of the Calendar window. All of the current calendars will be shown. Tap once on the **i** symbol next to a calendar, and select a new color as required.

73

Sharing music, books and movies

Family Sharing means that all members of the group can share purchases from the iTunes Store, the App Store or the Books app. To do this:

1 Open the **iTunes Store** app, the **App Store** app or the **Books** app

iTunes Store   App Store   Books

2 Access the **Purchased** section for the selected app. (For the **App Store**, tap once on the Account icon and tap once on the **Purchased** button; for the **iTunes Store**, tap once on the **Purchased** button on the bottom toolbar; for the **Books** app, tap once on the Account icon)

Hot tip

The Account icon in the App Store app and the Books app is the one containing the photo that you used for your Apple ID, located at the top of the window.

...cont'd

③ For all three apps, tap once on a member under the **Family Purchases** heading to view their purchases and download them, if required, by tapping once on this button

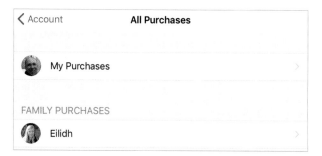

When the **Find My** app is opened, tap once on the **People** button to see people who have been added via Family Sharing. They must also have Location Services turned **On** (**Settings > Privacy > Location Services**) so that you can locate them. Tap once on the **Devices** button to view all of the Apple devices that can be located with the Find My app, including your own and those of any family members who have been added.

Finding family members

Family Sharing makes it easy to keep in touch with the rest of the family and see exactly where they are. This can be done with the Find My app. The other person must have their iPad (or other Apple device) turned on and be online. To find family members:

① Tap once on the **Find My** app

② The location of any people who are linked via your Family Sharing is displayed. Tap once on a person's name under

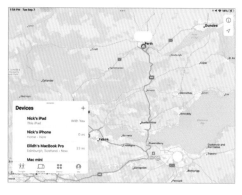

the **People** button (see tip) to view their location. Swipe outward with thumb and forefinger to zoom in on the map and see the precise location

4 Keyboard and Apple Pencil

The iPad has a virtual keyboard and can also be used with an external one. This chapter shows how to manage the keyboard, and the Apple Pencil, for entering text.

76   It's Virtually a Keyboard

78   Moving the Keyboard

79   Entering Text

80   Editing Text

82   Keyboard Settings

83   Using Predictive Text

84   Keyboard Shortcuts

86   Using the Apple Pencil

88   Voice Typing

It's Virtually a Keyboard

The keyboard on the iPad is a virtual one; i.e. it appears on the touchscreen whenever text or numbered input is required for an app. This can be for a variety of reasons:

- Entering text with a word processing app, email, or an organization app such as Notes.

- Entering a web address into a web browser such as the Safari app.

- Entering information into a form.

- Entering a password.

Viewing the keyboard

When you attempt one of the items above, the keyboard appears so that you can enter any text or numbers:

Around the keyboard

To access the various keyboard controls:

1 Tap once on the **Shift** button to create a **Cap** (capital) text letter

2 Double-tap on the **Shift** button to enable **Caps Lock**

3 Tap once on this button to back-delete an item

Don't forget

In addition to the iPad virtual keyboard, it is also possible to use a traditional computer keyboard with the iPad. This is the Apple Smart Keyboard (see page 13). Other physical keyboards are also available for use with the iPad, including the Apple Wireless Keyboard, which connects via Bluetooth. This can be turned on in the Settings app, under the Bluetooth tab.

Don't forget

To return from Caps Lock, tap again on the **Shift/Caps** button.

Additional buttons

In iPadOS 15, letters, numbers and symbols can all be accessed from a single keyboard. To do this:

1 Swipe down on one of the keys on the top line of the keyboard to enter the equivalent number, rather than a letter

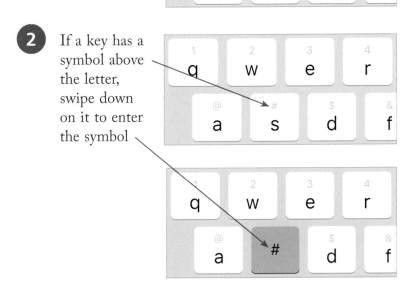

2 If a key has a symbol above the letter, swipe down on it to enter the symbol

3 Tap once on this button to hide the keyboard

If you are entering a password, or details into a form, the virtual keyboard will have a **Go** or **Send** button that can be used to activate the information that has been entered.

The virtual keyboard changes slightly according to the app you are using. For instance, in the Mail app, the keyboard differs depending on whether you are adding a recipient (the @ key appears on the keyboard) or adding body text.

Moving the Keyboard

By default, the virtual keyboard appears as a single unit along the bottom of the screen. However, it is possible to undock the keyboard and also split it to appear on either side of the screen. To do this:

Hot tip

The keyboard can also be split by swiping outward on both sides, with one finger on each side. Reverse the process to merge it again.

1 Press and hold this button on the keyboard

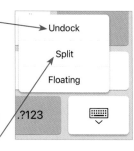

2 Tap once on the **Undock** button

3 The keyboard is undocked from the bottom of the screen and can be moved around the screen by pressing and holding on the button in Step 1

Hot tip

Floating mode for the keyboard can also be activated by pinching inward on the keyboard with two fingers. Swipe outward with two fingers to return it to its default state.

4 Tap once on the **Split** button in Step 2 to split the keyboard to the left and the right sides of the screen

5 Tap once on the **Floating** button in Step 2 to create a minimized version of the keyboard, which can be dragged around the screen using the bar at the bottom

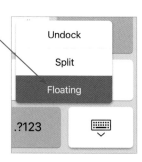

Hot tip

The floating keyboard can also be returned to its default state by dragging it to the bottom of the window.

6 To redock the keyboard, press and hold on the button in Step 1 and tap once on the required command

Entering Text

Once you have applied the keyboard settings that you require, you can start entering text. To do this:

1 Tap once on the text entry area to activate the keyboard. Start typing with the keyboard. The text will appear at the point where you tapped on the screen

2 If Predictive text is **Off**, as you type, Auto-Correction comes up with suggestions. Tap once on the spacebar to accept the suggestion, or tap once on the cross next to it to reject it

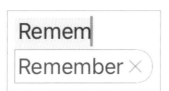

3 Any misspelled words appear underlined in red

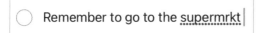

4 Tap once on this button to hide the keyboard

If Predictive text is **On**, the suggested word will appear above the keyboard on the QuickType bar (see page 83).

If you keep typing as normal, the Auto-Correction suggestion will disappear when you finish the word.

The virtual keyboard can be used for slide typing, when the text is added by swiping over the letters on the keyboard. This can be set up in **Settings > General > Keyboard** by turning **Slide on Floating Keyboard to Type** to **On**.

Editing Text

Once text has been entered it can be selected, copied, cut and pasted. Depending on the app being used, the text can also be formatted, such as with a word processing app.

Managing text

To work with text in a document you have created:

1 To change the insertion point in a document, press on the cursor to pick it up

Moving the cursor.

2 Drag the cursor to move the insertion point

Moving the cursor.

3 Tap once at the insertion point to access the menu buttons

| Select | Select All | Paste | Insert Drawing | **B**_I_U | Indentation |

Working with text on the iPad

4 Double-tap on a word to select it. Tap once on one of the menu buttons, as required

| Cut | Copy | Paste | Replace... | **B**_I_U | Look Up | Translate | Share... | Indentation |

Working with text on the iPad

5 Use the Shortcuts bar on the keyboard to, from left to right: cut the selection; copy the selection; or paste an item

Selecting text

Text can be selected using a range of methods:

1 Double-tap on a word to select it

Moving the cursor using iPadOS

2 Drag the selection handles to increase or decrease the selection. This is a good way to select certain text within a sentence or within a paragraph. (Text can also be selected by dragging on the selected word, rather than using the selection handles)

Moving the cursor using iPadOS

3 Triple-tap on a word to select the whole of its related paragraph

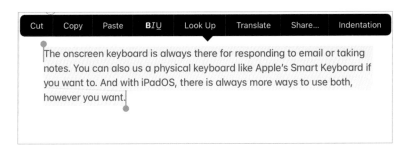

Cut	Copy	Paste	**B**_I_U	Look Up	Translate	Share...	Indentation

The onscreen keyboard is always there for responding to email or taking notes. You can also us a physical keyboard like Apple's Smart Keyboard if you want to. And with iPadOS, there is always more ways to use both, however you want.

Once text has been selected, there are a range of gestures that can be used to copy and paste it, and also undo the previous action. To copy selected text: pinch inward over the text with thumb and two fingers. To paste text: swipe outward with thumb and two fingers, in a dropping motion. To undo the previous action: swipe from right to left with three fingers.

The **Auto-Correction** function works as you type a word, so it may change a number of times, depending on the length of the word you are typing.

Don't forget

For more information about Text Replacement, see page 85.

Keyboard Settings

Settings for the keyboard can be determined in the **General** section of the Settings app. To do this:

1 Select **Settings > General** and tap once on the **Keyboard** option

Auto-Capitalization	
Auto-Correction	
Check Spelling	
Enable Caps Lock	
Shortcuts	

Keyboard

2 Drag the **Auto-Capitalization** button **On** to ensure letters will automatically be capitalized at the beginning of a sentence

3 Drag the **Auto-Correction** button **On** to ensure suggestions for words will appear as you type

4 Drag the **Check Spelling** button **On** to spell-check words as you type

5 Drag the **Enable Caps Lock** button **On** to enable this function to be performed

6 Drag the **"." Shortcut** button (further down the Keyboard settings screen) **On** to enable the functionality for adding a period/full stop with a double tap of the spacebar

7 Tap once on the **Keyboards** option to access options for adding different keyboards

Keyboards

Text Replacement

8 Tap once on the **Text Replacement** option to view existing text shortcuts and also to create new ones

Using Predictive Text

Predictive text tries to guess what you are typing, and also predicts the next word following the one you have just typed. It was developed primarily for text messaging, and it is included on the iPad with iPadOS 15. To use it:

1 Tap once on the **General** tab in the Settings app

2 Tap once on the **Keyboard** option

Keyboard

3 Drag the **Predictive** button **On**

4 When Predictive text is activated, the QuickType bar is displayed above the keyboard. Initially, this has a suggestion for the first word to include. Tap on a word, or start typing

Predictive text learns from your writing style as you write, and so gets more accurate at predicting words.

5 As you type, suggestions appear. Tap on one to accept it. Tap on the word within the quotation marks to accept exactly what you have typed, or tap on another option

6 After you have typed a word, a suggestion for the next word appears. This can be selected by tapping on it, or ignored

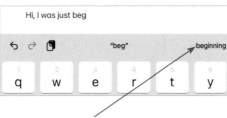

Keyboard Shortcuts

There are two types of shortcuts that can be used on the iPad keyboard:

- Shortcuts using keys on the keyboard

- Shortcuts created with text abbreviations

Shortcuts with keys

The shortcuts that can be created with the keys on the keyboard are:

Hot tip

The shortcut in Step 1 can be disabled by switching off the **"."** **Shortcut** option within the **Settings > General > Keyboard** section.

NEW

If you are using an external keyboard with your iPad, press and hold the **Command** (**cmd**) key to view a list of available keyboard shortcuts, which can be accessed with keystrokes on the keyboard, or by tapping once on a shortcut on the screen. This is a new feature in iPadOS 15.

1 Double-tap on the spacebar to add a full stop/period and a space at the end of a sentence

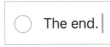

2 Swipe up once on the comma (or press and hold) to insert an apostrophe

3 Swipe up once on the full stop/period to insert quotation marks

4 Press and hold on appropriate letters to access accented versions for different languages

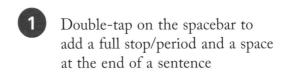

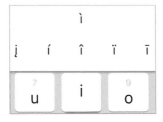

Text abbreviations

To create shortcuts with text abbreviations:

1 Tap once on the **Keyboard** option in the **General** section of the Settings app

Keyboard

Don't forget

The shortcut does not need to have the equivalent number of letters as words in the phrase. A 10-word phrase could have a two-letter shortcut.

2 Tap once on the **Text Replacement** option

Text Replacement

3 Tap once on this button to add a new shortcut

4 Enter the phrase you want to be made into a shortcut

Phrase   My name is Nick

5 Enter the abbreviation you want to use as the shortcut for the phrase

Shortcut   mnn|

Hot tip

To use a shortcut, enter the abbreviation. As you type, the phrase appears underneath the abbreviation. Tap once on the spacebar to add the phrase, or tap once on the cross to reject it. To delete a shortcut, in the **Text Replacement** section in Step 7, swipe on it from right to left and tap once on the **Delete** button.

6 Tap once on the **Save** button   Save

7 The shortcut is displayed here

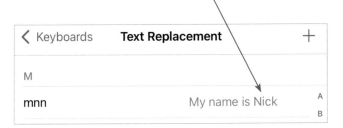

‹ Keyboards   **Text Replacement**   +

M

mnn   My name is Nick   A
                                          B

8 Use the Search box or the alphabetical bar at the right-hand side to search for other shortcuts that have been created

Using the Apple Pencil

The Apple Pencil is an excellent option for getting creative with drawing apps and it is also very effective in a range of text tasks, including converting handwriting, deleting text and selecting text.

Scribble
The Apple Pencil can be used to create handwritten text in compatible apps. In some cases this can then be converted automatically into typed text. This works in any text field and the text can then be edited in several ways. This is known as Scribble. To use Scribble with the Apple Pencil:

The Scribble option is activated in **Settings** > **Apple Pencil** by dragging the **Scribble** button **On**.

1 In a text box, or a Search box, use the Apple Pencil to enter handwritten text

2 When you finish writing a word, it will be converted to typed text, with relevant options displayed, depending on the text box in which it is entered

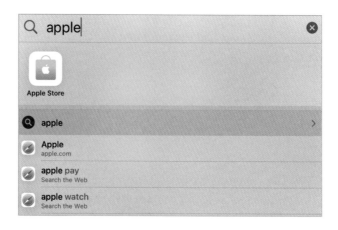

Deleting text

Text in a text field (including a web browser address bar) can be deleted using the Apple Pencil. This can be done if it is entered as handwriting and then converted to text, or entered directly from the keyboard:

1 Enter text into a text box or web browser

2 If there is a mistake in a word, scribble over it with the Apple Pencil

3 The word is deleted

Selecting text

The Apple Pencil can also be used to select text in a text field, after which editing options can be applied to it.

1 Circle the required text item with the Apple Pencil. This can be a single word, or several

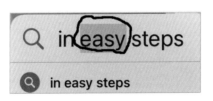

2 The circled text is selected and available editing options are displayed

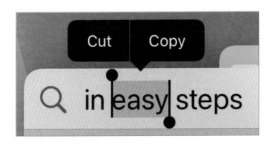

Hot tip

Press and hold with the Apple Pencil in any text field, to create a space to write or type another word.

Hot tip

Draw a line between letters to create a space between them, or draw a line in the space between two words to remove the space and join the words together.

Voice Typing

On the keyboard there is also a voice-typing option, which enables you to enter text by speaking into a microphone, rather than typing on the keyboard. This is On by default.

Using voice typing

Voice typing can be used with any app with a text-input function. To do this:

Beware

Voice typing is not an exact science, and you may find that some strange examples appear. The best results are created if you speak as clearly as possible and reasonably slowly.

1 Tap once on this button on the keyboard to activate the voice-typing microphone. Speak into the microphone to record text

2 As the voice-typing function is processing the recording, this screen appears

Hot tip

The first time that you tap on the **Microphone** button you may be prompted to select the **Enable Dictation** button too. This can also be done within **Settings > General > Keyboard > Enable Dictation**.

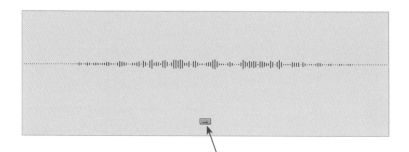

3 Tap once on the **Keyboard** button to finish recording and return to the virtual keyboard

4 Once the recording has been processed, the text appears in the app

Don't forget

There are other voice-typing apps available from the App Store. Two to try are Dragon Anywhere and Voice Dictation, Voice to Text.

Voice typing

Hello my name is Nick. Yes I was done with my voice.

5 Knowing your Apps

Apps keep the iPad engine running. This chapter details the built-in ones and shows how to review and download more through the App Store.

90 What is an App?

91 Built-in Apps

94 About the App Store

95 Finding Apps

97 Obtaining Apps

98 Updating Apps

99 Organizing Apps

100 Deleting Apps

You need an active internet connection to download apps from the App Store.

Hot tip

Within a number of apps there is a **Share** button that can be used to share items through a variety of methods, including email, messages, Facebook and Twitter. The **Share** button can also be used to share items using the AirDrop function over short distances with other compatible Apple devices (see page 38). To access these options, tap once on this button, where available:

What is an App?

An app is just a more modern name for a computer program. Initially, it was used in relation to mobile devices, such as the iPhone and the iPad, but it is now becoming more widely used with desktop and laptop computers, for both Mac and Windows operating systems.

On the iPad there are two types of apps:

- **Built-in apps**. These are the apps that come pre-installed on the iPad.

- **App Store apps**. These are apps that can be downloaded from the online App Store. There is a huge range of apps available there, covering a variety of different categories. Some are free, while others have to be paid for. The apps in the App Store are updated and added to on a daily basis, so there are always new ones to explore.

There are also two important points to remember about apps (both built-in and those from the App Store):

- Apart from some of the built-in apps, the majority of apps do not interact with each other. This means that there is less chance of viruses being transmitted from app to app on your iPad, and apps can also operate without a reliance on other apps.

- Content created by apps is saved within the app itself, rather than within a file structure on your iPad – e.g. if you create a note in the Notes app, it is saved there; if you take a photo, it is saved in the Photos app. Content is also usually saved automatically when it is created or edited, so you do not have to worry about saving as you work.

Built-in Apps

The built-in iPad apps are the ones that appear on the Home screen when you turn on the iPad:

- **App Store**. This can be used to access the App Store, from where additional apps can then be downloaded.

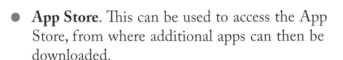

- **Books**. This is an app for downloading electronic books, which can then be read on the iPad. This can be done for both plain text and illustrated items.

- **Calendar**. An app for storing appointments, important dates and other calendar information. It can be synced with iCloud.

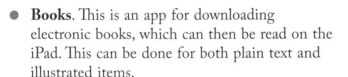

- **Camera**. This gives direct access to the front-facing and rear-facing iPad cameras. You can also access your Photos gallery from here.

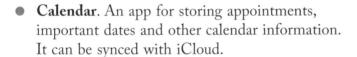

- **Clock**. This displays the current time and can be used to view the time in different countries, and also as an alarm clock and a stopwatch.

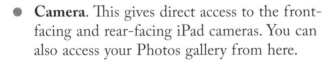

- **Contacts**. An address book app. Once contacts are added here they can then also be accessed from other apps, such as Mail.

- **FaceTime**. This is an app that uses the built-in front-facing camera on the iPad to hold video chats with other people with Apple devices, and also invite people who are using non-Apple devices (Windows or Android).

Some of the built-in apps appear on the second Home screen of the iPad.

The iPad **Settings** app is another of the built-in apps, and this is looked at in detail on pages 24-25.

You need an Apple ID to obtain content from the **Books** app. Books are downloaded in a matter of seconds, and you cannot change your mind once you have entered your Apple ID details. For full details about obtaining an Apple ID, see page 103.

...cont'd

- **Files**. This app can be used to display and access files held on your iPad, in iCloud Drive, and other online file storage services such as Dropbox.

- **Find My**. This is an app that can be used to view the location of anyone who is part of your Family Sharing group in iCloud, and also locate any other linked Apple devices.

- **Home**. This can be used to control certain compatible functions within the home, such as heating controls.

- **iTunes Store**. This app can be used to browse the iTunes store, where music, TV shows, movies, and more can be downloaded to your iPad.

- **Mail**. This is the email app for sending and receiving email on your iPad.

- **Maps**. Use this app to view maps from around the world, find specific locations, and get directions to destinations.

- **Measure**. This can be used to measure objects, using the iPad's camera.

- **Messages**. This is the iPad messaging service, which can be used between iPads, iPhones, iPod Touches and Mac computers. It can be used with not only text, but also photos and videos.

- **Music**. An app for playing music on your iPad and also accessing the Apple Music service, which connects to the whole iTunes Library.

- **News**. This is an app that collates news stories and content from numerous sources.

There have to be compatible devices in the home in order for the Home app to work with them. Check out **Smart Homes in easy steps** at www.ineasysteps.com for more help with this.

Some of the built-in apps, such as **Mail** and **Contacts**, interact with each other when required. However, since these are designed by Apple, there is little chance of them containing viruses.

...cont'd

- **Notes**. If you need to jot down your thoughts or ideas, this app is perfect for just that.

- **Photo Booth**. This is an app for creating fun and creative effects with your photos.

- **Photos**. This is an app for viewing and editing photos, creating slideshows, and for viewing the videos you have taken with your iPad camera. It can also be used to share photos via iCloud.

- **Podcasts**. This can be used to download and play podcasts from within the App Store.

- **Reminders**. Use this app for organization, when you want to create to-do lists and set reminders for events.

- **Safari**. The Apple web browser that has been developed for viewing the web on your iPad.

- **Stocks**. This can be used to display real-time stock prices and related news from Apple News.

- **Tips**. This can be used to display tips and hints for items on your iPad.

- **Translate**. This can be used to translate a wide range of different languages, including audio conversation options.

- **TV**. Previously called the Video app, this is an app for viewing videos purchased from the Apple TV Store on your iPad, and also streaming them to a larger HDTV monitor.

- **Voice Memos**. This can be used to record and share voice recordings.

It is worth investing in a good pair of headphones for listening to music and podcasts so that you do not disturb other people.

The Translate app is a new item in iPadOS 15.

93

About the App Store

While the built-in apps that come with the iPad are flexible and versatile, it really comes into its own when you connect to the App Store. This is an online resource containing thousands of apps that can be downloaded and then used on your iPad, including categories from Lifestyle to Travel.

To use the App Store, you must first have an Apple ID. This can be obtained when you first connect to the App Store. Once you have an Apple ID, you can start exploring the App Store:

For full details about obtaining an Apple ID, see page 103.

Tap once on the **Get** button to download a free app (a paid-for one will display a price).

The **Arcade** section is a monthly subscription service that contains an extensive range of games.

1 Tap once on the **App Store** app on the Home screen

2 The App Store Home screen (**Today**) displays the latest current recommended apps, on a daily basis. Swipe up the page to move to other daily recommendations, including the Daily List

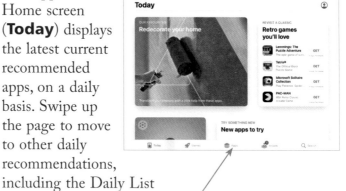

3 Tap on the buttons on the bottom toolbar to view the apps according to **Today**, **Games**, **Apps**, and **Arcade**

4 Tap once on an app to view its details

5 Swipe up the page to view more information about the app

Finding Apps

Within the App Store, apps are separated into categories according to type. To find apps in the App Store:

1 Tap once on the **Apps** button on the bottom toolbar

2 Details of the latest apps are displayed

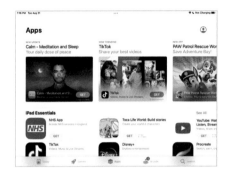

Some apps will differ depending on the geographical location from where you are accessing the App Store.

3 Scroll down the page (by swiping up) to view the different sections. Tap once on the **See All** button to view all of the items in a section

You can buy bundles of apps from some developers at a reduced price.

Categories

To view the different categories in the App Store:

1 Tap once on the **Apps** button on the bottom toolbar

2 Swipe up the page to the **Top Categories** section

Top Categories

- Entertainment
- Graphics & Design
- Productivity
- Kids
- Education
- AR Apps

When viewing apps within a specific category, swipe up the page to view the **Top Paid** and **Top Free** apps for the category.

3 Tap once on the **See All** button to view all of the available categories. Tap once on a category to view the apps within it

...cont'd

Don't forget

Another way to find apps is with the App Store Search button, which is located at the right of the bottom toolbar of the App Store. To use this: tap once on the Search button

Q Search

and tap once in the Search box to bring up the iPad virtual keyboard. Enter a search keyword or phrase. Suggestions appear as you are typing. Tap once on a result to view the related app and information about it.

Beware

Do not limit yourself to just viewing the top apps. Although these are the most popular, there are also a lot of excellent apps within each category.

Top Charts

To find the top-rated apps:

1 Tap once on the **Apps** button on the bottom toolbar

2 Swipe up the page to view the current **Top Paid Apps** and **Top Free Apps**

3 Tap once on the **See All** button to see the full range of paid-for and free apps

See All

4 Tap once on the **All Apps** button, and tap once on a category to view the Top Paid and Top Free apps for that category

All Apps

Obtaining Apps

When you identify an app that you would like to use, it can be downloaded to your iPad. To do this:

1 Find the app you want to download, and tap once on the button next to the app (this will say **Get** or will have a price)

2 Tap once on the **Install** button

3 The app will begin to download onto your iPad, indicated by this icon next to it in the App Store

4 Once the app is downloaded it will appear in the next available space on one of the Home screens. Tap once on the app to open and use it

Apps usually download in a few minutes or less, depending on the speed of your internet connection.

Some apps have "in-app purchases". This is additional content that has to be paid for when it is downloaded.

You should keep your apps as up-to-date as possible to take advantage of software fixes and updates.

Hot tip

If updates are not set to be downloaded automatically, a notification badge will appear on the App Store icon to indicate that updates are available. These can then be updated in the **Account** section of the App Store, under the **Available Updates** heading.

Hot tip

The notification badge on apps (such as the **App Store** and the **Mail** app) can be turned On or Off in **Settings** > **Notifications** > **[select app]** by dragging the **Badges** button **On** or **Off**.

Updating Apps

The world of apps is a dynamic and fast-moving one, and new apps are being created and added to the App Store on a daily basis. Existing apps are also being updated, to improve their performance, security and functionality. Once you have installed an app from the App Store, it is possible to obtain updates at no extra cost (whether or not the app was paid for). To do this:

1 Set updates to be downloaded automatically: **Settings** > **App Store** > and drag **App Updates** to **On**

2 Tap once on the **App Store** app

3 In the App Store, tap once on the **Account** button, located at the top right-hand side of the screen

4 Tap once on the **Purchased** button

5 Tap once on the **Open** button to open the latest version. (If automatic updates have not been selected, there will be an **Update All** option at the bottom of the window in Step 4 for apps for which there are updates)

Organizing Apps

When you start downloading apps you will probably soon find that you have dozens, if not hundreds, of them. You can move between screens to view all of your apps by swiping left or right with one finger. It is also possible to organize apps into individual folders to make using them more manageable. To do this:

Hot tip

To move an app between screens, press and hold on it until it starts to wobble and a minus sign appears in the corner. Then, drag it to the side of the screen. If there is space on the next screen, the app will be moved to the point at which it is released.

1 Press on an app until it starts to wobble and a cross appears at the top-left corner

2 Drag the app over another one

Beware

Only top-level folders can be created; i.e. sub-folders cannot be created. Also, one folder cannot be placed within another.

3 A folder is created, containing the two apps. The folder is given a default name, usually based on the category of the apps

4 Tap on the folder name, and type a new name if required

Hot tip

If you want to rename an apps folder after it has been created, press and hold on it until it starts to wobble. Then, tap on it once and edit the name, as in Step 4.

5 Click the **Home** button once to finish creating the folder, and click it again to return to the Home screen. The folder is added to the Home screen. Tap once on this to access the items within it

Deleting Apps

If you decide that you do not want certain apps anymore, they can be deleted from your iPad. However, they remain in iCloud so that you can reinstall them if you change your mind. This also means that if you delete an app by mistake, you can get it back from the App Store without having to pay for it again. To delete an app:

Beware

If you delete an app it will also delete any data that has been compiled with that app, even if you reinstall it from the App Store.

1 Press on an app until it starts to wobble and a minus sign appears at the top-left corner

2 Tap once on the minus sign to delete the app. In the Delete dialog box, tap once on the **Delete App** button. The app is then uninstalled from your iPad

Remove "iTunes U"?
Removing from Home Screen will keep the app in your App Library.

Delete App

Remove from Home Screen

Cancel

To reinstall an app:

Don't forget

In iPadOS 15 some, but not all, of the built-in apps can be deleted. This is done in the same way as for deleting an app, shown on this page.

1 Tap once on the **App Store** app

App Store

2 Tap once on the **Search** button on the bottom toolbar

Q Search

3 Enter the name of the app in the Search box, and tap once on the **iCloud** icon to download it again

iTunes U
Free educational courses
★★★☆☆ 577

6 Keeping in Touch

This chapter shows how to use your iPad to keep ahead in the fast-moving world of online communications, using email, a range of texting options, and video chatting with the updated FaceTime app.

102 Getting Online

103 Obtaining an Apple ID

104 Setting up an Email Account

105 Emailing

106 Text Messaging

108 Enhancing Text Messages

109 Shared with You

110 Video Chatting with FaceTime

115 Adding Social Media

116 Communication Apps

Getting Online

iPads can be used for a variety of different communications, but they all require online access. This is done via Wi-Fi, and you will need to have an Internet Service Provider (ISP) and a Wi-Fi router to connect to the internet. Once this is in place, you will be able to connect to a Wi-Fi network.

If you have the cellular version of the iPad you can obtain internet access this way, but this has to be done through a provider of this service, as with a cell/mobile phone.

1 Tap once on the **Settings** app

2 Tap once on the **Wi-Fi** tab

3 Ensure the **Wi-Fi** button is in the **On** position

4 Available networks are shown here. Tap once on yours to select it

5 Enter the password for your Wi-Fi router

If you are connecting to your home Wi-Fi network, the iPad should connect automatically each time, once it has been set up. If you are connecting in a public Wi-Fi area, you will be asked which network you would like to join.

6 Tap once on the **Join** button

7 Once a network has been joined, a check mark appears next to it. This now provides access to the internet

Obtaining an Apple ID

An Apple ID is an email address and password registered with Apple that enables you to log in and use a variety of online Apple services. These include:

- App Store

- iCloud

- Messages

- FaceTime

- iTunes Store and Apple Music

- Books

It is free to register for an Apple ID, and this can be done when you access one of the apps or services that require it, or you can register on the Apple website at Apple ID (**https://appleid.apple.com**):

1 Tap once on the **Create Your Apple ID** button at the top of the Apple ID web page

Create Your Apple ID

2 Enter the details for the Create Your Apple ID wizard to set up your Apple ID Account. (If you are using an Apple ID to buy items using Apple apps and services, you will need to provide a valid method of payment)

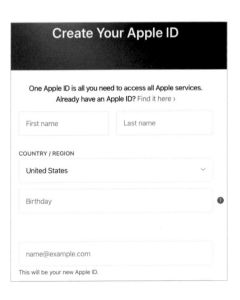

Create Your Apple ID

One Apple ID is all you need to access all Apple services.
Already have an Apple ID? Find it here ›

First name | Last name

COUNTRY / REGION

United States

Birthday

name@example.com

This will be your new Apple ID.

Hot tip

Settings > Apple ID, iCloud, Media & Purchases is where you can access your Apple ID details.

Hot tip

The Apple ID settings (above) also include account recovery options, where you can specify a contact who can be used to recover your Apple ID account details, and also a Recovery Key that can be used to restore the data on your iPad. Find these at **Settings > Apple ID, iCloud, Media & Purchases > Password & Security > Account Recovery**.

Setting up an Email Account

Email accounts

Email settings can be specified within the Settings app. Different email accounts can also be added. To do this:

Hot tip

If you don't already have an email account set up, you can choose one of the providers from the list and you will be guided through the setup process.

Hot tip

If your email provider is not on the **Add Account** list, tap once on **Other** at the bottom of the list and complete the account details using the information from your email provider.

Don't forget

If you set up more than one email account, messages from all of them can be downloaded and displayed by **Mail**.

1 Tap once on the **Settings** app

2 Tap once on the **Mail** tab

3 Tap once on the **Accounts** button
Accounts

4 Tap once on the **Add Account** option to add a new account

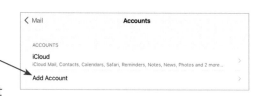

5 Tap once on the type of email account you want to add

6 Enter your login details for the account. Follow the wizard for the account, and tap on the **Next** button at each stage

Emailing

Email on the iPad is created, sent and received using the Mail app. This provides a range of options for managing email, including adding mailboxes and viewing email conversation threads.

Accessing Mail

To access Mail, and start sending and receiving emails:

1 Tap once on the **Mail** app (the red icon in the corner displays the number of unread emails in your Inbox)

2 Tap once on a message to display it in the main panel

3 Use these buttons to, from left to right: delete the current message, move it to another folder, or create a new message

4 Tap once on this button, at the bottom right of the Mail window to reply to a message, forward it to a new recipient, delete it, move it to another folder, or mark it as read or unread

Hot tip

To quickly delete an email from your Inbox, swipe on it from right to left and tap once on the **Trash** (Delete) button. This also generates an option to **Flag** the email, and a **More** button from which you can reply, forward, mark or move the current email.

Hot tip

Use the email settings (**Settings** > **Mail**) to access numerous options for customizing how the Mail app operates.

Don't forget

Once an email has been written, tap once on this button to send it to the recipient:

Don't forget

You need an Apple ID to send iMessages, and have to sign in with it when you start using the Messages app.

Don't forget

iMessages are sent using Wi-Fi. If a Wi-Fi connection is not available, the message cannot be sent, unless the iPad has a cellular network connection.

Don't forget

If an iPad has a cellular network connection then this can be used to send regular text messages to other compatible devices such as cell/mobile phones. If the recipient is not using iMessages, the message will be sent as a standard SMS (Short Message Service). By default, iMessages appear in blue bubbles and SMS messages in green bubbles.

Text Messaging

Text messaging should not be thought of as the domain of the younger generation. On your iPad you can join the world of text with the Apple iMessage service that is accessed via the Messages app. This enables text, photo, video, emojis and audio messages to be sent, free of charge, between users of iPadOS on the iPad, iOS on the iPhone and iPod Touch, and Mac computers. iMessages can be sent to cell/mobile phone numbers and email addresses.

1 Tap once on the **Messages** app

2 Tap once on this button to create a new message and start a new conversation

3 Tap once on this button to select someone from your contacts

4 Tap once on a contact to select them as the recipient of the new message

5 Tap once in the text box, and type with the keyboard to create a message. Tap once on this button to send the message

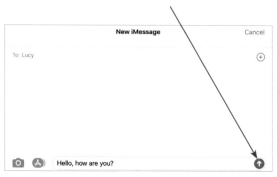

6 As the conversation progresses, each message is displayed in the main window

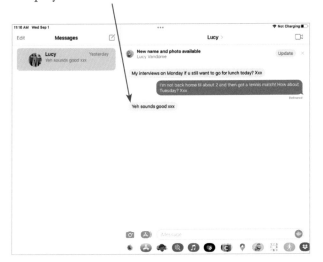

Press and hold on a message, and tap on the **More...** button that appears. Select a message, or messages, and tap on the **Trash** icon to remove them.

7 To edit whole conversations, tap once on the **Edit** button in the Messages panel

Edit

When a message has been sent, you are notified underneath it when it has been delivered.

8 Tap once on **Select Messages**

Select Messages	⊘
Edit Pins	🖈
Edit Name and Photo	◉

9 Tap once here to select the conversation, and tap once on the **Delete** button at the bottom of the page to delete the conversation

Delete

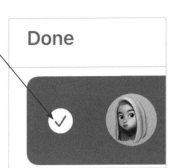
Done

Press and hold on a name in the Messages panel and tap once on the **Pin** button to pin this conversation to the top of the panel.

Pin 🖈

Enhancing Text Messages

Adding emojis

Emojis (small graphical symbols) can be used with the Messages app:

Emojis can be added automatically to replace certain words. Add text, and tap once on the **Emoji** button in the first Step 1. Any items that can be replaced by an emoji are highlighted. Tap once on the highlighted word to add an emoji.

1 Tap once on this button on the keyboard to view the emoji keyboards

2 Swipe left and right to view the emoji options. Tap once on an emoji to add it to a message

iMessages can also be sent with certain animated effects:

1 Write a message and press and hold on this button

2 Tap once on the **Bubble** button at the top of the window, and tap once on one of the options. These are **Slam**, which creates a message that moves in  at speed from the side of the screen; **Loud**, which creates a message in large text; **Gentle**, which creates a message in small text; and **Invisible Ink**, which creates a message that is concealed and then reveals the text

Tap once on the Camera icon on the bar below the text box to take a photo to add to a message, or tap once on the Photos icon to add a photo from the Photos app.

3 Repeat Step 1 for Bubble effects and tap once on the **Screen** button at the top of the window. Swipe left and right to view the full-screen effects. Tap once on this button to send the message

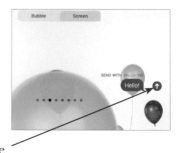

Shared with You

Text messages that you receive with the Messages app can contain a range of content other than text, including photos, audio clips, links to news items, links to websites, and music. When you receive this type of content, it can be downloaded to your iPad and you will be able to access it from the relevant app, using Shared with You – e.g. the Photos app for photos or video, Safari for web links, and so on. The apps that support Shared with You are: Photos, Safari, News, Music, Podcasts and Apple TV. To use Shared with You:

1 Open one of the apps that is compatible with Shared with You and tap once on this button to access the app's sidebar (this example is for the Photos app)

2 Tap once on the **For You** button (or **Shared with You** in some apps)

3 The **Shared with You** section contains any compatible items that have been sent to you via the Messages app

Shared with You

From **Lucy** >

4 The sender of the shared item is listed next to it. Tap once on their name to reply via a text message, without having to first open the Messages app

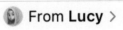

From **Lucy** >

Beware

The Apple TV app does not have a sidebar, but the Shared with You items can be accessed from the **Library** button on the bottom toolbar.

NEW

If numerous photos are sent to you in the Messages app, they will all be available in the For You section of the Photos app. In addition, they can also be viewed in **Grid** view in the Messages app itself, by tapping once on this button next to the photos:

7 Photos

This is a new feature in iPadOS 15.

Video Chatting with FaceTime

Video chatting is a very personal and interactive way to keep in touch with family and friends around the world. To use FaceTime for video chatting:

The FaceTime app has been comprehensively updated in iPadOS 15.

Don't forget

To make video calls with FaceTime you need an active internet connection and to be signed in with your Apple ID.

1 Tap once on the **FaceTime** app

2 Tap once on the **New FaceTime** button

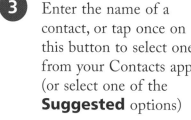

3 Enter the name of a contact, or tap once on this button to select one from your Contacts app (or select one of the **Suggested** options)

4 Use the Contacts app to select a contact

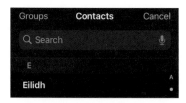

5 Tap once on the **FaceTime** video button to make a FaceTime call (to another FaceTime user: the **Create Link** in Step 2 can be used to make FaceTime calls to non-FaceTime users – see page 113)

110

6 If a contact is added directly into the **To** box in Step 2 on the previous page, tap once on the **FaceTime** button to start a video call with them

Beware

7 When you have connected, your contact appears in the main window and you appear in a Picture in Picture thumbnail in the corner

Although it was not included with the original release of iPadOS 15, the SharePlay option, for viewing movies and listening to music with other people on a FaceTime call, will be included with subsequent updates to iPadOS 15. This includes a SharePlay button on the control panel in Step 8. See page 114 for details.

8 Use these buttons during a call to, from left to right: send a text message to one of the people on the FaceTime call; turn the speakers on or off; mute or unmute the microphone; turn the camera on or off for the call (audio will still be available if the camera is off); and end the call

9 Tap once on the **FaceTime Video >** button in Step 8 to access more options for the call, including, from top to bottom: ending the call; adding more people to the call; sharing links to the call for non-FaceTime users; and silencing requests from other people to join a FaceTime call

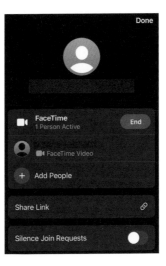

Hot tip

The **Share Link** option in Step 9 can be used to create FaceTime calls with non-FaceTime users, including those using the Windows and Android operating systems. See page 113 for details.

Don't forget

When you receive a FaceTime call, it appears as a small banner at the top of the screen.

Spatial sound is used in group calls to present the sound as coming from the direction of the screen in which someone's FaceTime window is positioned, to create a more natural effect. This is available on iPads with the A12 Bionic chip, and later, and is a new feature in iPadOS 15.

Voice isolation is a new feature in iPadOS 15.

...cont'd

Receiving a FaceTime call

To answer a FaceTime call made to you from someone else:

1 Tap once the green video button to accept the call, or tap once on the red button to decline the call

2 After either of the options in Step 1 has been selected, tap once on the **Accept** button, or tap once on the **Remind Me** button, to get a reminder about the call instead of answering it

3 Tap once on the **Message** button in Step 2 to send a text message instead of answering a call

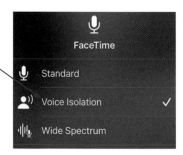

Microphone modes

FaceTime also has options for how the microphone operates:

1 Start a FaceTime call, access the Control Center (see page 38) and tap once on the **Mic Mode** button

2 Tap once on the **Voice Isolation** button to block out background noise and give clearer prominence to the current speaker in a call

Creating a FaceTime link

Before iPadOS 15 it was only possible to use FaceTime to make video calls to other FaceTime users who were using an Apple device. However, that has now changed and the functionality of FaceTime has been expanded considerably, with the inclusion of an option to send a link to anyone, who can then join the FaceTime call via the web. To do this:

Creating links for users without the FaceTime app to join a FaceTime call is a new feature in iPadOS 15.

1 Open the FaceTime app and tap once on the **Create Link** button

It is also possible to invite someone to an existing FaceTime call, via a link, using the **Share Link** button in Step 9 on page 111.

2 Select an option for how you want to send the link to join the FaceTime call – e.g. by email

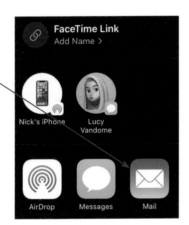

When someone receives an invitation to a FaceTime call, the recipient can tap once on the **FaceTime Link** button in the invitation, enter their name and tap once on the **Continue** button.

3 Compose an invitation in the app selected in Step 2 and send it to the recipient

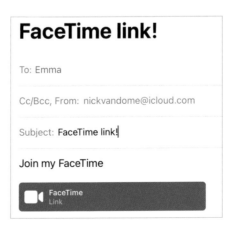

113

...cont'd

Using SharePlay in FaceTime

SharePlay is a function within FaceTime that enables you to share your screen, and to play movies and TV shows or play music, and share this content with other people on a FaceTime call. To do this:

Beware

Although SharePlay was announced as part of iPadOS 15, it was not included in the original release of the operating system. However, it will be included in subsequent updates to iPadOS 15, which can be downloaded from **Settings** > **General** > **Software Update**.

Don't forget

Skype and Zoom are other options for making free video calls to other Skype or Zoom users. The apps can be downloaded from the App Store.

1 Access **Settings > FaceTime** and drag the SharePlay button **On**

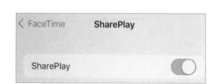

2 Start a FaceTime call and tap once on this button on the FaceTime control panel to share your iPad screen with everyone else on an existing a call

3 Tap once on the **Share My Screen** button

4 To share a movie or TV show, or music tracks, open them in either the Apple TV app or the Music app respectively, and tap once on the **SharePlay** button

5 Tap once on the **SharePlay** button to play the selected item for everyone in the FaceTime call

6 When SharePlay is being used, this button is visible at the top of the FaceTime window

Adding Social Media

Using social media sites such as Facebook, Instagram and Twitter to keep in touch with family and friends has now become common across all generations. On the iPad with iPadOS 15, it is possible to download a range of social media apps and also view updates through the Notification Center (see second Hot tip). To add social media apps:

Social media websites can also be accessed directly through the Safari web browser.

1 Open the App Store and navigate to the **Apps** > **Categories** > **Social Networking** section

 Social Networking

2 Tap once on the required apps to download them to your iPad

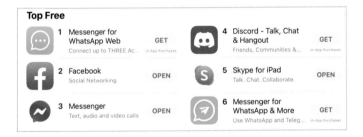

Top Free

1 Messenger for WhatsApp Web — Connect up to THREE Ac... — **GET** — In-App Purchases	4 Discord - Talk, Chat & Hangout — Friends, Communities &... — **GET** — In-App Purchases	
2 Facebook — Social Networking — **OPEN**	5 Skype for iPad — Talk. Chat. Collaborate. — **OPEN**	
3 Messenger — Text, audio and video calls — **OPEN**	6 Messenger for WhatsApp & More — Use WhatsApp and Teleg... — **GET** — In-App Purchases	

See page 116 for more about social networking apps.

3 Tap once on an app to open it

 Facebook

4 If you already have an account with the social media service, enter your login details, or tap once on the **Sign Up** button to create a new account

Phone number or email

Password

Log In

Sign Up for Facebook   Need Help?

Social media updates for some apps can be set to appear in your **Notification Center**. Open **Settings** and tap once on the **Notifications** tab. Under the **Notification Style** heading, tap once on the social networking site and select options for how you would like the notifications to appear.

On Facebook you can have private text conversations with your friends, as well as posting public information for all of your friends to see. For more information, check out **Facebook for Seniors in easy steps** in our online shop at www. ineasysteps.com

When you follow people on Twitter, their Tweets appear on your Homepage feed. If they are very prolific, or you follow a lot of people, this may result in a lot of messages to read. You can turn off notifications for individual apps if you wish – see page 54.

Communication Apps

Within the App Store there is a range of communication apps that can be used to contact friends and family via text, phone and video. There are also several apps for sharing information, updates and photos. Some of these are:

- **Facebook**. The social networking phenomenon that has over a billion users around the world. This app enables you to create and use a Facebook account from your iPad. You can then interact with friends and family by posting messages, comments and photos.

- **Twitter**. Another one of the top social networking sites on the web. It provides the facility to post text or news messages (Tweets) of up to 280 characters. You can choose other users to follow, so you see their Tweets, and other people can follow you to see yours, too.

- **Snapchat**. This is a popular photo- and video-sharing app: items can be shared for a limited period of time and they are then deleted.

- **Instagram**. Another very popular photo- and video-sharing app, used by people to document every part of their lives and activities.

- **Flickr**. An iPad version of the popular photo- and video-sharing site. You have to register for an account, and once you have done this you can share your photos and videos with a vast online community.

- **Skype**. The widely-used service for making video and voice calls. This is free when both users are using Skype over Wi-Fi. Skype can also be used for text messaging.

- **Zoom**. Another popular app for making video and voice calls to family and friends.

- **WordPress**. A web publishing app that can be used to create online blogs and your own websites.

- **Gmail**. If you have a Gmail account this will enable you to access it directly from your iPad.

7 On a Web Safari

This chapter shows how to use the functionality of the built-in iPad web browser, Safari, to access the web and start enjoying the benefits of the online world.

118 Around Safari

120 Safari Settings

121 Navigating Pages

122 Sidebar

123 Bookmarking Pages

124 Tab View

125 Opening New Tabs

126 Web Page Options

Around Safari

The Safari app is the default web browser on the iPad. This can be used to view web pages, bookmark pages, and read pages with the Reader function. To start using Safari:

1 Tap once on the **Safari** app

2 Tap once on the Address Bar at the top of the Safari window. Type a name or a web page address

3 Tap once on the **Go** button on the keyboard to open the web page that was entered, or select one of the options below the Address Bar

4 The selected page opens with the top toolbar visible. As you scroll down the page, this disappears to give you a greater viewing area. Tap on the top of the screen, or scroll back up to display the toolbar again

...cont'd

5 Swipe up and down and left and right to navigate around the page

6 Swipe outward with thumb and forefinger to zoom in on a web page (pinch inward to zoom back out)

When a page opens in Safari, a blue status bar underneath the Address Bar indicates the progress of the loading page.

Double-tap with one finger to zoom in on a page by a set amount. Double-tap again with one finger to return to normal view. If the page has been zoomed by a greater amount by pinching, double-tap with two fingers to return to normal view.

Other browsers can be downloaded from the App Store. Some to try are: Google Chrome; Dolphin Web Browser; Firefox; and Opera Browser.

Safari Settings

Settings for Safari can be specified in the Settings app.

Beware

If other people have access to the iPad, don't use **AutoFill** for names and passwords for any sites with sensitive information, such as banking sites.

Hot tip

If the **Open New Tabs in Background** option in Step 4 is set to **On**, you can press and hold a link on a web page and select **Open in New Tab**. The link then opens in a new tab behind the one you are viewing.

Don't forget

Cookies are small items from websites that obtain details from your browser when you visit a site. The cookie remembers the details for the next time you visit the site.

1 Open the Settings app and tap once on the **Safari** tab

2 Tap once on the **Search Engine** link to select a default search engine to use

> Search Engine

3 Tap once here for options for filling in online forms

> GENERAL
>
> AutoFill

4 Drag this button **On** to open new pages in the background of your current page

> Open New Tabs in Background

5 Drag this button **On** to keep the Favorites Bar in view under the Address Bar in Safari

> Show Favorites Bar

6 Drag the **Block All Cookies** button **On** or **Off** as required

> Block All Cookies

7 Tap once on **Clear History and Website Data** to remove these

> Clear History and Website Data

8 Drag this button **On** to enable alerts for when you visit a fraudulent website

> Fraudulent Website Warning

9 Drag this button **On** to block pop-up messages

> Block Pop-ups

Navigating Pages

When you are viewing pages within Safari there are a number of functions that can be used:

1 Tap once on these arrows to move forward and back between web pages that have been visited

2 Tap once here to view Shared with You items, bookmarked pages, Reading List pages and browsing history (see page 122)

3 Tap once here to add a bookmark (see page 123); add to a Reading List; add an icon to your iPad Home screen; email a link to a page; share using social media, messaging and other apps; or print a page

4 Tap once here to open a new tab (see page 125)

5 Tap and hold a link to access additional options, including: Open; Open in Background; Open in Tab Group; Open in Split View; Download Linked File; Add to Reading List; Copy; or Share using a selection of options

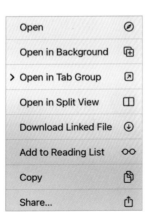

Open	⊘
Open in Background	⊞
> Open in Tab Group	↗
Open in Split View	⊓
Download Linked File	⊕
Add to Reading List	∞
Copy	🗐
Share...	⬆

6 Tap and hold on an image, and tap once on **Share...**, **Add to Photos** or **Copy**

Share...	⬆
Add to Photos	⬇
Copy	🗐

Hot tip

Tap and hold on the **Forward** and **Back** arrows in Step 1 to view lists of previously-visited pages in these directions. See page 123 for more on bookmarking.

Hot tip

Files can be downloaded from Safari and then viewed in the Files app, from the Downloads button in the sidebar. To do this, press and hold on a link on a web page to the file you want to download, and tap once on the **Download Linked File** button.

Download Linked File	⊕

Sidebar

The Safari sidebar can be used to manage the tabs within Safari, use private browsing, and also view items that have been saved within Safari. To use the sidebar:

The Safari sidebar has been updated in iPadOS 15.

1 Tap once here to view or hide the sidebar

2 Tap once on the **Tabs** button to view all of the currently-open tabs in Safari

Tap once on this button in the top right-hand corner of the sidebar to access options for creating a new, empty tab group or one from the existing tabs.

3 Tap once on the **Private** button to access web pages without any browsing data being recorded or stored

4 Tap once on the **Shared with You** button to view web pages that have been shared with you, via the Messages app. See page 109 for details

5 Tap once on the **Bookmarks** button to view web pages that have been bookmarked – see the next page for details

To add an item to the Reading List, access the required web pages and tap once on this button on the top toolbar to access the sharing options. Tap once on the **Add to Reading List** button.

6 Tap once on the **Reading List** button to view items that have been saved to be read offline

7 Tap once on the **History** button to view your web browsing history

Bookmarking Pages

Once you start using Safari, you will soon build up a collection of favorite pages that you visit regularly. To access these quickly, they can be bookmarked so that you can go to them in one tap. To set up and use bookmarks:

1 Open a web page that you want to bookmark. Tap once on this button on the top toolbar to access the sharing options

2 Tap once on the **Add Bookmark** button

For pages that you access frequently, you can also choose to **Add to Home Screen** from the sharing options in Step 2 (swipe up the panel to access this option).

123

3 Tap once in this box to select whether to include the bookmark on the Favorites bar or in a Bookmarks folder

4 Tap once on the **Save** button

5 On the web page, tap once to access the sidebar. Tap once on the **Bookmarks** button to view all of the bookmarks that have been added

Tab View

Tabs can be managed using iPadOS 15 on the iPad so that you can view all of your open Safari tabs on one screen, including those on other compatible Apple devices. To do this:

1 Tap once here to activate **Tab View**

2 All of the currently-open tabs are displayed. Tap on one to open it

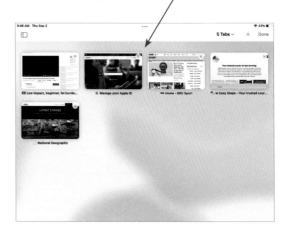

3 Tap once the **Tabs** button on the top toolbar to access options for viewing Private tabs and also for creating new tab groups

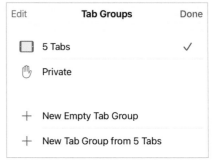

Opening New Tabs

Safari supports tabbed browsing, which means that you can open separate pages within the same window and access them by tapping on each tab at the top of the page:

1 Tap once here to open a new tab for another page

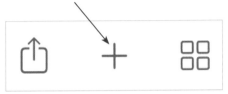

2 Open a new page by entering a web address into the Address Bar, or tap on one of the thumbnails in the **Favorites** window

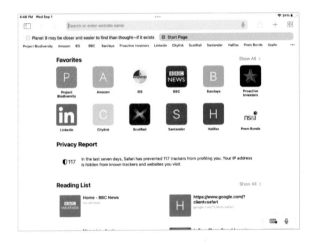

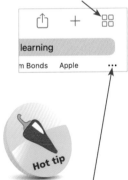

3 Tap once on the tab headings to move between tabbed pages

4 Tap once on the cross to the top left of a tab to close the active tab

Web Page Options

Being able to view web pages in the way that you want is an important part of any browsing experience, and Safari offers various options for displaying web pages. These can be accessed from the left-hand side of the Address Bar:

Don't forget

In Reader View, the button in the Address Bar turns black. Tap once on it to access options for how Reader View is displayed, including text size, background color and font. It can also be used to hide Reader View and return to the full web page.

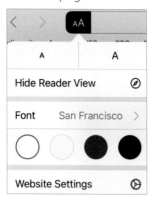

1 Tap once on this button in the Address Bar

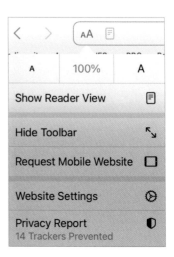

2 The web page options are displayed

3 Tap once on these buttons to change the text size of a web page

4 Tap once on the **Show Reader View** button to view the current web page with just text and no extra content, such as adverts

5 Tap once on the **Hide Toolbar** button to hide the toolbar and create a larger viewing area for the current web page

6 Tap once on the **Request Mobile Website** button to view a mobile version of the website, if there is one

7 Tap once on the **Website Settings** button to access settings for the website being viewed

Hot tip

Tap once on the **Privacy Report** button in Step 3 to view details of items that have been blocked.

8 Staying Organized

An iPad is ideal for organizational tasks. This chapter shows how to keep fully up-to-date with notes, calendars and reminders.

128 Taking Notes

132 Quick Notes

134 Setting Reminders

136 Using the Calendar

138 Your iPad Address Book

139 Printing Items

140 Organization Apps

Taking Notes

It is always useful to have a quick way of making notes of everyday things, such as shopping lists, recipes or packing lists. On your iPad, the Notes app is perfect for this:

1 Tap once on the **Notes** app

2 Tap once on this button to create a new note

3 Tap once in the text area of a new note to access the keyboard. Start writing the note

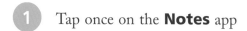

Formatting notes

To apply a range of formatting to a note:

1 Press and hold next to the piece of text you want to format. Tap once on the **Select** button

2 Drag the yellow selection handles over the text you want to select

Don't forget

If iCloud is set up for Notes (check **Notes** is **On** in **Settings** > **Apple ID iCloud, Media & Purchases** > **iCloud**) then all of your notes will be stored here and will be available on any other iCloud-enabled devices that you have.

Don't forget

The title for a note is taken from the first line of text that is entered.

3 Tap once on the **Formatting** button on the Shortcuts bar above the keyboard to access the formatting options, including text styles such as the Title, Heading or Body options, or list options for creating a list from the selection

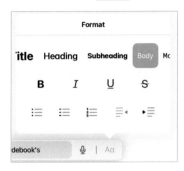

4 Tap once on the **List** button on the top toolbar to create a checklist from the selected text. Radio buttons are added to the list (these are the round buttons to the left-hand side of the text). Tap once on the radio buttons to show that an item or a task has been completed

5 Tap once on the **Camera** button on the top toolbar and tap once on the **Take Photo or Video** button to add a photo or a video to the note, or tap once on the **Choose Photo or Video** button to add a photo from the iPad's photo library

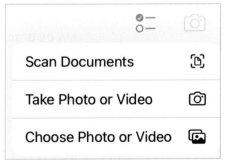

Options for formatting text in a note are located on the Shortcuts bar, below the main text window, and on the top toolbar.

Items in a list can be set to automatically move to the bottom of the list once they have been completed. To do this, go to **Settings** > **Notes** > **Sort Checked Items** and tap once on the **Automatically** option.

Tap once on this button on the Shortcuts bar to insert a table into a note:

...cont'd

Tap once on the menu button in the top right-hand corner of the Notes panel to access a menu for managing your notes, including: changing the Notes window view; selecting notes; sorting notes; and viewing any attachments that have been added to notes.

Notes can also be deleted by swiping from right to left on them in the Notes panel and tapping once on the Trash icon.

6 Tap once on the **Add Sketch** button to add a freehand sketch to a note. Click on the pen and color options as required

7 Tap once on this button on the keyboard to hide the keyboard and finish the note. To edit an existing note, tap once on the text and the keyboard will reappear

Managing notes

Once notes have been created they can be managed from within their own window. To do this:

1 In the main Notes window, tap once on the menu button, at the right-hand side of the top toolbar

2 Tap once on the menu options to apply them. These include options for: scanning items into a note; pinning a note; locking a note; or deleting it. There are also options for: sharing or sending the current note; searching for items; moving a note to a folder within the Notes app; applying lines and grids over a note; and printing a note

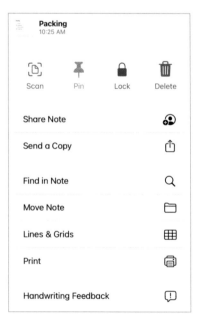

Pinning notes

By default, the most recently-created or edited note appears at the top of the Notes panel. However, it is possible to pin your most frequently-used notes to the top of this panel. To do this:

1 Press and hold on the note to be pinned

2 Tap once on the **Pin Note** button

3 The note is pinned at the top of the Notes panel. Tap once here to show or hide pinned notes

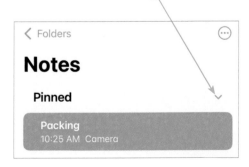

Don't forget

To unpin a note, press and hold on it and tap once on the **Unpin Note** button.

Quick Notes is a new feature in iPadOS 15.

Hot tip

A Quick Note button can be added to the Control Center, so Quick Notes can be started from here. To do this, access **Settings** > **Control Center** and under the **More Controls** heading, tap once on the green button next to the **Quick Note** option.

Don't forget

The title of a Quick Note is taken from the first line of text. If no text is entered, the title will be **New Note**.

Quick Notes

The functionality of the Notes app has been expanded with iPadOS 15, so that notes can be created from within any other app without having to open the Notes app separately. This is known as Quick Notes. Once these have been created, they are all stored in the Notes app. To create and manage Quick Notes:

1. From within any app, swipe inward from the bottom right-hand corner of the iPad

2. The Quick Note panel appears

3. Enter the text for the Quick Note, or write with an Apple Pencil, and tap once on the **Done** button

4. Tap once on the **Notes** app to open it

5. The Quick Note is available in the left-hand sidebar and can be opened in the same way as a regular note – i.e. by tapping once on it

6 When creating a
Quick Note, use these
buttons at the top of

the window to, from left to right: view all Quick
Notes in context within the Notes app; access the
Quick Notes menu, which has options for sharing
the Quick Note, adding a link to it (for an item such
as a web page), and deleting the Quick Note; and
creating a new Quick Note

Adding links

Links can be added to Quick Notes, from the currently-
active app, for some apps. One option is to add a link to a
web page. To do this:

1 Open a web page in the Safari app and create a new
Quick Note, as shown in Step 1 on the previous
page. The currently-active web page is referenced at
the top of the Quick Note

2 Tap once on the **Add Link** button to add it to the
Quick Note. The link is added to the Quick Note.
Tap once on the link to access the linked item

The apps that can be
used to add links to
Quick Notes include
Safari, Mail, Messages
and Maps. Photos can
also be added to a
Quick Note by opening
the Photos app,
accessing a Quick Note
and dragging a photo
into the note.

Once content has
been added to a Quick
Note, it can then be
accessed from the
Quick Note in the
Notes app – i.e. if a
web link has been
added, tap once on
the link in the Quick
Note to go to the
linked web page.

Setting Reminders

Another useful organization app is Reminders. This enables you to create lists for different topics and then set reminders for specific items. A date and time can be set for each reminder, and when this is reached, the reminder appears on your iPad screen. To use Reminders:

Hot tip

Reminders is one of the apps that can also be used with the online iCloud service, which is provided once you have an Apple ID. This is accessed at **www.icloud.com** Other apps that can be accessed here include Contacts, Calendar and Notes.

Hot tip

If Family Sharing has been set up (see page 71 for details), you can create a family reminder that will appear for all members of your Family Sharing circle. To do this, tap once on the **Family** button in Step 2 and add a reminder in the usual way.

1. Tap once on the **Reminders** app

2. The items that have been created are listed under specific categories and beneath the **My Lists** heading. This includes reminders and lists. Tap once on the **Edit** button to reorder or delete any of the lists

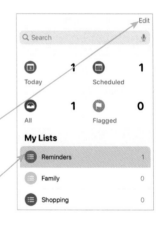

3. Tap once on the Reminders option and tap once on the **New Reminder** button

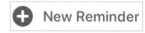

4. Enter details of the reminder and tap once on the **i** button to access the **Details** window

5 Drag the **Date** or **Time** buttons **On** and select options for relevant items for the reminder

6 Tap once on the **Done** button to create the reminder

7 On the date and time of the reminder, a pop-up box appears

8 Press on the reminder to expand the box. Tap once on **Mark as Completed** to close the reminder, or select an option for being reminded about it

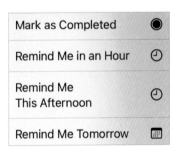

9 Tap once on the **Today** and **Scheduled** buttons at the top left-hand side of the main app window (shown in Step 2 on the previous page) to see reminders and lists for these categories. Appropriate items will be added automatically to these categories

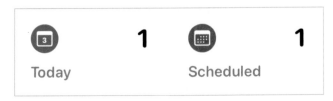

For a recurring reminder, tap once on the **Repeat** link in the **Details** window in Step 4 on the previous page (if a date and time have been set), and select a repeat option from: Never, Hourly, Daily, Weekly, Biweekly, Monthly, Every 3 Months, Every 6 Months, or Yearly. The reminder will then appear at the specified time and date set in Step 5.

Hot tip

135

Using the Calendar

The built-in iPad calendar can be used to create and view appointments and events. To do this:

Don't forget

The iPad calendar uses continuous scrolling to move through Month view. This means you can view weeks across different months, rather than just viewing each month in its entirety; i.e. you can view the second half of one month and the first half of the next one in the same calendar window.

Don't forget

Drag the **All-day** button **On** to set an event for the whole day.

1. Tap once on the **Calendar** app

2. By default, the calendar is displayed in **Month** view. Swipe up and down to move between weeks and months

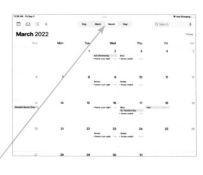

3. Tap once here to view the calendar by **Day**, **Week**, **Month** or **Year** view

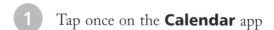

4. Tap once on the **Today** button to view the current date

5. Tap once on this button to create a new event, or press and hold on a different date to add an event here

6. Enter a title and a location for the event

7. Drag the **All-day** button **Off** to set a timescale for the event

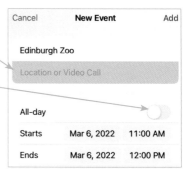

8 Tap on the **Starts** and **Ends** dates to set these

A new event can also be created in **Day** view. Press and hold on a time slot to access the **New Event** window.

9 To invite other people to the event, tap once on the **Invitees** link (Calendars needs to be **On** in iCloud for this function)

10 Tap once on this button to select a contact from your address book

Tap once on the **Repeat** link in the **New Event** window to set a recurring event, such as a birthday. The repeat options are Every Day, Every Week, Every 2 Weeks, Every Month, or Every Year.

137

11 The contact is added as an invitee for the event

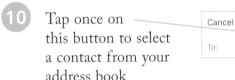

12 Tap once on the **Done** button. An email invitation will then be sent to the invitee's email address

13 Tap once on the **Add** button shown in the image for Step 6 when you have finished entering the details of the event

14 Press and hold on an event, and tap on the **Edit** button to alter the details of the event

Select an event to edit as in Step 14, and tap once on the **Delete Event** button at the bottom of the window to remove it.

Delete Event

Your iPad Address Book

There is a built-in address book on your iPad: the Contacts app. This enables you to store contact details, which can then be used to contact people via email, iMessage or FaceTime. To add contacts:

1 Tap once on the **Contacts** app

2 Tap once on this button to add a new contact

3 Enter the required details for a contact

The details of an individual contact can be shared via email or as an iMessage, using the **Share Contact** button at the bottom of their entry.

Share Contact

4 Tap once on the **Done** button Done

5 Use these buttons to send a text message, make a call, start a FaceTime video call or send an email to the contact

6 Tap once on the **Edit** button to edit details in an individual entry Edit

7 To delete a contact, swipe to the bottom of the window in Edit mode and tap once on the **Delete Contact** button Delete Contact

138

Printing Items

Printing from an iPad has advantages and disadvantages. One advantage is that it is done wirelessly, so you do not have to worry about connecting wires and cables to a printer. The main disadvantage is that not all printers work with the iPad printing system.

AirPrint

Content from an iPad is printed using the AirPrint system that is part of the iPadOS 15 operating system. This is a wireless printing system that connects to your printer through your Wi-Fi network. However, not all printers are AirPrint- or Wi-Fi-enabled, so it may not work with your current printer.

AirPrint can print content from apps with the Share button, including built-in apps like Safari, Notes, Mail, and Photos:

Check on the Apple website for a list of AirPrint-enabled printers: **https:// support.apple.com/ en-us/HT201311**

1 Tap once on the **Share** button and tap once on the **Print** button

> Print

2 Tap once here to select your AirPrint printer

Cancel	**Print Options**	Print
Printer		No Printer Selected >
1 Copy		— +

3 Select options for the number of copies, double- or single-sided, and color, then tap once on the **Print** button

Cancel	**Print Options**	Print
Printer		HP ENVY 4500 series [FAE7FA] >
1 Copy		— +
Paper Size		Double-sided, Color >

Apps in the Apple productivity suite – Pages, Numbers and Keynote – contain the **Print** button within the **More** options that are accessed from the top toolbar.

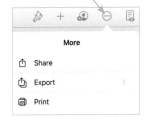

Organization Apps

In the App Store there is a wide range of productivity and organization apps. Some of these are:

- **Evernote**. One of the most popular note-taking apps. You can create individual notes and also save them into notebook folders. Evernote works across multiple devices, so if it is installed on other computers or mobile devices, you can access your notes wherever you are.

- **Popplet**. This is a note-taking app that enables you to link notes together so that you can form a mindmap-type creation. You can also include photos and draw pictures.

- **Dropbox**. This is an online service for storing and accessing files. You can upload files from your iPad and then access them from other devices with an internet connection.

- **Bamboo Paper**. This is another note-taking app, but it allows you to do this by handwriting rather than typing. The free version comes with one notebook into which you can put your notes, and the paid-for version provides another 20.

- **Pages**. This is a powerful word processing app that has been developed by Apple. It can be used to create and save documents, which can then be printed or shared via email. There are a number of templates on which documents can be based. There is also a range of formatting and content options.

- **Keynote**. Another Apple productivity app, this is a presentation app that can be used to create slides, which can then be run as a presentation.

- **Numbers**. This is the spreadsheet app that is part of the same suite as Pages and Keynote. Again, templates are provided, or you can create your spreadsheets from scratch to keep track of expenditure or household bills, for instance. You can enter formulas into cells to perform simple or complicated calculations.

Most organization apps are found in the **Productivity** category of the App Store.

Other productivity and organization apps to look at include: Notability; Alarmed; AnyList: Grocery Shopping List; OfficeSuite; iA Writer; Smartsheet; and GoodReader PDF Editor & Viewer.

9 Leisure Time

The possibilities for enjoyment from your iPad are huge. This chapter looks at listening to music, capturing and editing photos, reading books, and keeping up with the news. It also covers some lifestyle apps including art, health, cookery, and games.

142 Buying Music and More

144 Playing Music

146 Taking Photos and Videos

147 Photos Settings

148 Viewing Photos

151 Editing Photos

152 Reading Books

154 Getting the News

156 Viewing Movies and TV Shows

157 Art and Drawing

158 Cooking with your iPad

159 Staying Healthy

160 Playing Games

Buying Music and More

As well as using the Music app (see pages 144-145), music on the iPad can also be accessed using the iTunes Store, using your Apple ID with credit or debit card details added. Music can then be played via the Music app:

1 Tap once on the **iTunes Store** app

2 Tap once on the **Music** button on the iTunes toolbar at the bottom of the window

Music can also be found and previewed from the **Browse** button in the **Music** app. Items can then be bought by tapping once on the **Buy on iTunes Store** button.

3 Scroll up and down to view the featured items, or tap once on the **Genres** button to find items this way

4 Tap once on an item to view it. Tap once here to buy an album, or tap on the price button next to a song to buy that individual item

5 Purchased items are included in the Music app's Library (see pages 144-145) as well as the iTunes Library, from where they can be downloaded again at any time to your iPad or any other Apple device

Around the iTunes Store

In addition to music there is a wide range of other content that can be downloaded from the iTunes Store:

Don't forget

1 Tap once on the **Movies** button to view the latest movie releases

 Movies

Scroll up and down to view the content on the Homepage for Movies and TV. Swipe left and right on individual panels to view the items in each section. Tap once on the **See All** button at the top of a panel – e.g. Recent Releases – to view all of the items within it.

2 Tap once on the **TV Shows** button to view the latest TV releases

 TV Shows

143

Hot tip

3 Tap once on the **Top Charts** button on the bottom toolbar to view the top-selling items for music, movies and TV

 Top Charts

4 Tap once on the **Genius** button on the bottom toolbar to view suggestions made by iTunes based on your previous purchases

Genius

5 Tap once on the **Purchased** button on the bottom toolbar to view all of your previous purchases from the iTunes Store

 Purchased

Since all items that you buy and download from the iTunes Store are kept within the Purchased section, if you ever delete or lose an item you can download it again, for free, from this section. Tap once on the cloud icon next to an item to download it again.

Hot tip

To create a playlist of songs, tap once on the **Playlists** button in the left-hand panel,

Playlists

then tap once on the **New Playlist** button. Give it a name, and then you can add songs from your Library.

Hot tip

Another music option is Apple Music. This is a subscription service that makes the entire Apple iTunes Library of music available to users. Music can be streamed over the internet, or downloaded so you can listen to it when you are offline. Apple Music can be accessed from the **Listen Now** button in the left-hand panel of the Music app.

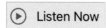

Playing Music

Once music has been bought from the iTunes Store it can be played on your iPad using the Music app. To do this:

1   Tap once on the **Music** app

2   Tap once on the **Library** button in the left-hand panel

3   Select one of the options for viewing items in the Library. This can be **Recently Added**, **Artists**, **Albums**, **Songs** or **Genres**

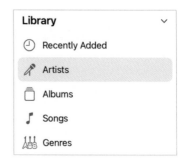

4   For the **Artists** section, tap once on an artist in the left-hand panel to view related items in the right-hand panel

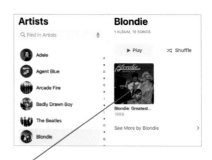

5   Tap once on an item in the right-hand panel to view its details. The tracks from the album are displayed

6 Tap once on a track to play it. Limited options for the music controls are displayed at the bottom of the window. Tap once here to view details of a track

Hot tip

Tap once on the **Browse** button in the left-hand sidebar to preview music from the iTunes Store. Items can then be bought from the iTunes Store, if required, from a link in the Browse section.

Browse

7 The details of the track are displayed. Use these buttons to rewind, pause/play and fast-forward the track

Don't forget

By default, music that has been bought from the iTunes Store is kept online and can be played on your iPad by streaming it online over Wi-Fi. However, it is also possible to download tracks to your iPad so that you can play them without being online. Tap once on this button to download a track:

8 Tap once on this button to access the menu for the currently-playing track. This includes sharing the song, downloading it onto your iPad, deleting it, adding it to a playlist, or sharing it

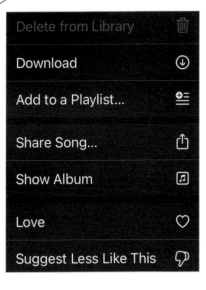

Delete from Library
Download
Add to a Playlist...
Share Song...
Show Album
Love
Suggest Less Like This

Taking Photos and Videos

The iPad is excellent for taking and displaying photos. Photos can be captured directly using one of the two built-in cameras (one on the front and one on the back) and then viewed, edited and shared using the Photos app.

Don't forget

The camera on the back of the iPad is capable of capturing high-resolution photos and also high-definition videos. The front-facing one is better for video calls and "selfies" (photos of yourself).

Beware

If you do not want to take a Live Photo, make sure that the button in Step 4 is **Off**.

Hot tip

Photos can also be taken with the Camera app by pressing either of the **Volume** buttons on the side of the iPad.

1 Tap once on the **Camera** app

2 Tap once on the shutter button to capture a photo

3 Tap once on this button to swap between the front and back cameras on the iPad

4 Tap once on this button on the top camera toolbar to take a Live Photo, which is a short, animated video in GIF file format. Live Photos can be played in the Photos app by pressing and holding on them to view the animated effects

The main iPad camera can be used for different formats:

1 Swipe up or down at the side of the camera screen, to access the shooting options. Tap once on the **Photo** button to capture photos at full-screen size. Tap once on the **Square** button to capture photos at this ratio. Tap once on the **Pano** button (accessed by scrolling past the Square option) to create panorama shots

2 Tap once on the **Video** button in Step 1, and press the red shutter button to take a video. Press the shutter button again to stop recording

Photos Settings

iCloud sharing

Certain photo options can be applied within Settings. Several of these are to do with storing and sharing your photos via iCloud. To access these:

1 Tap once on the **Settings** app

2 Tap once on the **Photos** tab

3 Drag the **iCloud Photos** button **On**

iCloud Photos	⬤

to upload your whole photo Library from your iPad to iCloud (it remains on your iPad too). Similarly, photos on your other Apple devices can also be uploaded to iCloud

4 Select an option for storing iCloud photos

Optimize iPad Storage	✓
Download and Keep Originals	

(**Optimize iPad Storage** uses less storage as it uses smaller file sizes of your images on your iPad, although the original file sizes are retained in iCloud)

5 Drag the **Shared Albums** button **On** to enable sharing your albums with family and friends, and also to be able to see their shared albums

Shared Albums	⬤

In the **Camera** settings, drag the **Grid** button **On** to place a grid over the screen when you are taking photos with the camera, if required. This can be used to help compose photos by placing subjects using the grid.

Check out these **In Easy Steps** titles to help you take great photos with your iPhone: Smartphone Photography in easy steps and 100 Top Tips – Create Great Photos Using Your Smartphone. Visit www.ineasysteps.com for more details.

Viewing Photos

Photos section

Photos can be viewed and organized in the Photos app. There are different sections for displaying photos in different ways. All photos can be viewed in the Photos section:

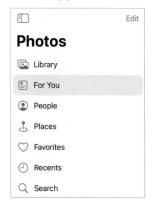

Photos

- 🖼 Library
- 📇 For You
- 👤 People
- ⚲ Places
- ♡ Favorites
- 🕐 Recents
- 🔍 Search

Edit

1 Tap once on the **Photos** app

2 Tap once on this button in the top left-hand corner of the Photos app to show or hide the sidebar

3 Tap once on the **Library** button in the sidebar and tap once on the **Years**, **Months**, **Days** or **All Photos** buttons to view your photos according to these criteria

4 In any of the categories, double-tap on a photo to view it at full size

...cont'd

For You section
The For You section is where the best of your photos are selected and displayed automatically. To use this:

1 Tap once on the **For You** button on the sidebar

2 The **For You** section contains **Memories**, **Shared with You**, **Featured Photos**, **Shared Albums** and **Sharing Suggestions**

For more details about the Shared with You feature, see page 109.

149

3 Memories are collections of photos created by the Photos app, using what it determines are the best shots for a related series of photos

4 Tap once on a slideshow to access the control buttons for playing or pausing the slideshow and displaying the photos in the Memory in a grid

...cont'd

Albums section

Albums can also be created to store similar photos:

Photos can be selected to enable options to be applied to them, such as being added to an album. To do this, access Days or All Photos in the Library section and tap once on the **Select** button. Tap on the photos you want to select, or drag over a range of photos.

Select

1 Access the **My Albums** section within the sidebar

2 Tap once on the **New Album** button at the bottom of the My Albums section

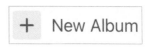

3 Enter a name for the new album and tap once on the **Save** button

Shared albums can be created in a similar way to standard ones. To do this, access the **Shared Albums** section in the sidebar and tap once on the **New Shared Album** button. Enter a name for the album and then invite people to view it, so it becomes shared. Photos can then be added to the album.

4 Tap once on the photos to be added to the album, and tap once on the **Done** button in the top right-hand corner of the window

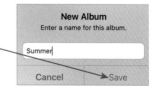

Search options

Items can be searched for in the Photos app by tapping once on the **Search** button in the sidebar. Suggested areas are displayed. Tap once on an item to see the photos within it, or enter a keyword or phrase into the Search box to search for specific items.

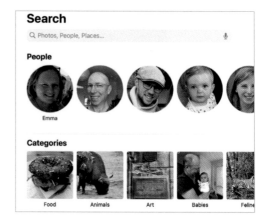

Editing Photos

The Photos app has options to perform a range of photo-editing operations. To use these:

1 Open a photo at full-screen size and tap once on the **Edit** button in the top right-hand corner

2 The main editing buttons are located on the left-hand side of the screen. These are for, from top to bottom: color adjustment, filters, and rotation and cropping

3 Tap once on one of the main editing buttons to view its options at the right-hand side of the screen

4 For the **Adjust** options, each item has a slider that can be used to change the level of the color adjustment

BRIGHTNESS

5 The **Filter** option has a range of filter effects at the right-hand side of the screen. Tap once on one of these to apply it to the photo

VIVID WARM

6 For the **Rotate** option, there are choices for how to rotate a photo; e.g. horizontally or vertically

7 Tap once on the **Done** button in the top right-hand corner to apply any editing changes that have been made

Don't forget

The color options in the Adjust section include: Auto, Exposure, Brilliance, Contrast, Brightness, Saturation, and Tint.

Hot tip

The **Photo Booth** app is a good one to use with grandchildren, who will enjoy experimenting with its fun and special effects. Open the app, select one of the effects, and take a photo as normal.

Photo Booth

Reading Books

For anyone interested in reading, the iPad removes the need to carry around a lot of bulky books. Whether you are at home or traveling, you can keep hundreds of digital books (ebooks) on your iPad. This is done with the Books app, which can be used to download and read books across most genres, like a portable library. To use Books:

The **Browse Sections** option in the Book Store contains links to a range of options, including **New & Trending**, **Top Charts**, **Bestsellers** and **Rave Reviews**. Tap on a category to view its content.

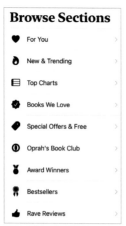

1 Tap once on the **Books** app

2 The Books app opens at the **Reading Now** section, which consists of any items that you have downloaded, and suggested titles

3 Tap once on the **Book Store** button on the bottom toolbar to access titles that can be bought and downloaded to the Books app (see the next page)

4 Tap once on the **Browse Sections** button in the top left-hand corner of the Book Store Homepage to view items according to different categories (see tip)

Once you have identified appropriate books in the Book Store, they can then be downloaded to the **Library** section of the Books app. To do this:

1 Tap once on the book image or title to view its details

2 View the details of the book, including a description. Scroll down the page to view more details about the book

3 Tap once on the **Buy** (or **Get**) button to purchase and download the book. Downloaded books appear in the **Library** section of the Books app

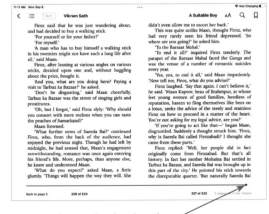

4 Tap once on a book thumbnail in the Library to open it. Tap on the page to access the controls.

Drag here to move through the book

Hot tip

Tap once on the **Want To Read** button in Step 3 to add the book as a suggested item under the Reading Now section. Tap once on the **Sample** button to read a sample directly from the Book Store.

Hot tip

Tap once on the left-hand and right-hand edges in Step 4 to move back or forward by one page.

Hot tip

Tap once on this button on the top toolbar in Step 4 to view the table of contents. Tap once on these buttons to, from left to right: change the text style and color; search for a word or phrase; and bookmark a page.

Getting the News

The News app is a news-aggregation app that collates news stories from a variety of publications, covering a range of categories. To use the News app:

1 Tap once on the **News** app

2 Tap once on the **Today** button in the sidebar to view the current news stories

Tap once on this icon to show or hide the sidebar:

3 The current news stories, based on your news feed, are displayed in the main window

4 Tap once on the **Edit** button to the right of the **Search** box

5 Your current news feed items can be removed by tapping on the red circle next to them. The order of importance can be rearranged by dragging these buttons. Tap once on the **Done** button

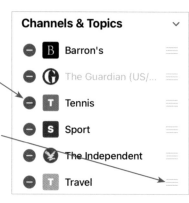

6 Scroll to the bottom of the left-hand panel, as displayed

Discover Channels

in Step 3 on the previous page, and tap once on the **Discover Channels** button

Hot tip

7 Suggested channels and topics are displayed. These can be added to your news feed by tapping once on the **+** icon next to an item. Tap once on the **Done** button

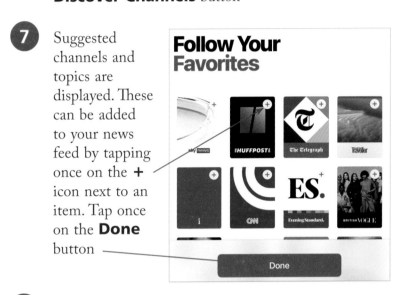

Follow Your Favorites

Done

Below the **Channels & Topics** heading in Step 3 is a **Suggested by Siri** heading that contains topics based on Siri searches. Tap once on the **+** icon to add a topic to your news feed.

Suggested by Siri	⌄
H Health	+
N NHS	+
S Science	+

8 Tap once on a news item in Step 3 on the previous page to view it in detail

9 When an item has been opened for reading, tap on these buttons on the top toolbar to, from left to right: bookmark an item; change the text size of an article; or access the menu for additional options, such as for sharing the item

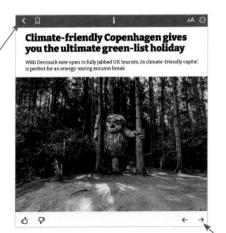

Climate-friendly Copenhagen gives you the ultimate green-list holiday

With Denmark now open to fully jabbed UK tourists, its climate-friendly capital is perfect for an energy-saving autumn break

Don't forget

Scroll down the **Follow Your Favorites** page in Step 7 to view more topics.

Hot tip

Tap once on these arrows to move between the next and previous news stories.

⟨ ▢   i   AA ☺

Viewing Movies and TV Shows

The TV app can be used to download and view movies and TV shows from the Apple TV service. There is no subscription for using the TV app on the iPad, but individual items usually require a payment to buy or rent them.

If you rent videos from the TV app you have to watch them within 30 days. Once you have started watching a video, you have to finish watching it within 48 hours. Once the rental period has expired, the video is deleted from the iPad.

The TV app can also be used to access the Apple TV+ service. This is a subscription service for streaming original TV shows and movies from Apple TV. There is a 7-day free trial and then the service costs $4.99 a month in the US and £4.99 in the UK.

1 Tap once on the **TV** app

2 Tap once on the **Watch Now** button on the bottom toolbar. Options for  accessing the available content are displayed. Swipe up and down the page to view the content, and tap once on the **See All** button to view all of the items within a category

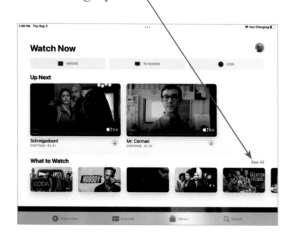

3 Tap once on the **Movies**, **TV Shows** and **Kids** buttons at the top of the 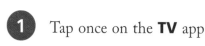 window to view items in these categories and download them

4 Tap once on the **Library** button on the bottom toolbar to view all of the items that you have downloaded from the TV app

Art and Drawing

Viewing art

It is always a pleasure to view works of art in real life, but the next-best alternative is to be able to look at them on the high-resolution Retina Display on your iPad. As far as viewing art goes, there are two options:

- Using apps that contain general information about museums and art galleries.

- Using apps that display the works belonging to museums and art galleries.

In general, type the name of a museum or art gallery into the App Store Search box to see if there is an applicable app.

Creating pictures

If you want to branch out from just looking at works of art, you can try creating some of your own too. There are a range of drawing and painting apps that can be used to let your creative side run riot. Most of these function in a similar fashion in terms of creating pictures, with drawing tools that you can select and then use to create a drawing by using your finger on the screen (or an Apple Pencil). Most drawing apps also have an Undo function and an Eraser to remove unwanted items. Some apps to try are:

- **Brushes Redux**. One of the most powerful painting apps with a wide range of tools and features, including up to six layers in each painting and five blend modes.

- **Drawing Pad**. Similar to Brushes Redux, but not at such a high level. Suitable as a starter option for iPad painting.

- **Inspire Pro**. A wide range of blending features makes this one of the best painting apps around.

- **How to Draw Everything Easy**. A drawing app that has tutorials for learning how to draw, and also examples that can be used as templates and copied over.

- **Sketch.Book – Draw, Drawing Pad**. A sketching app at a similar level to Brushes Redux, for painting.

Most top museums have some form of app available. If there is not one for a museum in which you are interested, try contacting the museum and ask if they are planning on developing an app.

If you cannot find a certain app in the search results in the App Store, tap once on the **Filters** button, to the left of the Search box, and select the **Supports > iPhone Only** option. These apps can be downloaded for the iPad too, although they will have a smaller screen area to view the app.

Cooking with your iPad

Your iPad may not be quite clever enough to cook dinner for you, but there are enough cookery apps to ensure that you will never go without a good meal with your iPad at your side. Some to look at are:

- **Allrecipes Magazine**. Packed full of recipes, step-by-step guides and cooking ideas, from the world's largest online community of chefs.

- **Change4Life Smart Recipes**. Over 160 healthy and tasty recipes for all meals throughout the day. There are also options for creating shopping lists and saving favorite recipes that you have created.

- **BigOven Recipes & Meal Planner**. Over 350,000 recipes to keep you busy in the kitchen for as long as you want. You can also store your grocery lists here.

- **Cake Recipes**. To get your mouth watering, this app has hundreds of cake ideas, from the simple to the exotic.

- **Green Kitchen**. A must for vegetarians, with stylish and creative recipes for organic and vegetarian food.

- **Vegan Recipes - Tasty Food**. An app featuring a comprehensive range of vegan recipes, including options for creating shopping lists and step-by-step guides to preparing tasty vegan meals.

- **Healthy Slow Cooker Recipes**. Put your dish together with this app, leave it in the slow cooker, and then enjoy it several hours later when ready.

Staying Healthy

Most people are more health-conscious these days, and usefully the App Store has a category covering health and fitness. This includes apps about general fitness, healthy eating, relaxation and yoga. Some to try are:

- **MyFitnessPal**. If you want to stick to a diet, this app can help you along the way. You need to register, which is free, and then you can set your own diet plan and fitness profile.

- **Daily Workouts Fitness Trainer**. Some of the exercise apps are for dedicated gym-goers. If you are looking for something a bit less extreme, this app could fit the bill. A range of easy-to-follow exercises that will keep you fit.

- **Yoga: Daily Yoga for Everyone**. Audio and video instructions for all levels of yoga enthusiasts.

- **Simple Meal Planner**. A dieting aid that enables you to create your own menu plans.

- **My Pilates Guru Lite**. Use this app to work through over 80 Pilates exercise sessions. You can also create your own sessions and save them to repeat.

- **Relax Melodies: Sleep Sounds**. Over 50 sound files to help you relax or fall asleep. Different melodies can be combined to create a customized soundtrack to help you get to sleep.

55 million
DOWNLOADS

Sleep better tonight

- **Pillow: Sleep Cycle Tracker**. An app that tracks your sleep, and its quality, to try to ensure that you get the best night's sleep possible.

- **Universal Breathing**. Designed to promote slow breathing, to enhance relaxation and general health.

Don't forget

There is also a **Medical** category in the App Store that contains a range of apps covering varied medical topics and subjects.

Beware

The iPhone also has a built-in Health app. However, this is not provided with the iPad, as it is designed to work with the iPhone and the Apple Watch. Find out more in our companion book **iPhone & Apple Watch for Health & Fitness in easy steps**.

Beware

If you have a genuine medical complaint, get it checked out by your doctor, rather than searching online.

Playing Games

Although computer games may seem like the preserve of the younger generation, this is definitely not the case. Not all computer games are of the shoot-em-up or racing variety, and the App Store also contains puzzles and versions of popular board games. Some games to try are:

As well as the games here, there is a full range of other types of games in the App Store, which can be accessed from the **Games** button on the bottom toolbar of the App Store.

160

For serious game players, the Arcade option in the App Store is worth looking at. This is accessed from the bottom toolbar in the App Store, and is a monthly subscription service. It includes all of the latest Apple games, which you can play on your own or against other people, including those in your Family Sharing group.

- **Chess**. Pit your wits against this Chess app. Various settings can be applied for each game, such as the level of difficulty.

- **Checkers**. Similar to the Chess app, but for Checkers (Draughts). Hints are also available to help develop your skills and knowledge.

- **Mahjong**. A version of the popular Chinese game, this is a matching game for single players, rather than playing with other people.

- **Scrabble GO**. An iPad version of the best-selling word game that can be played with up to four people.

- **Solitaire**. An old favorite, the card game where you have to build sequences and remove all of the cards.

- **Sudoku**. The logic game where you have to fill different grids with numbers 1-9, without having any of the same number in a row or column.

- **Tetris**. One of the original computer games, where you have to piece together falling shapes to make lines.

- **Words With Friends**. Similar to Scrabble, an online word game, played with other users.

10 Traveling Companion

This chapter shows how the iPad is an essential travel accessory. It looks at the Maps app for getting around, and a range of travel apps.

162 Looking Around Maps

164 Getting Directions

166 Traveling with your iPad

167 Planning your Trip

168 Viewing Flights

169 Finding Hotels

170 Converting Currency

171 Travel Apps

To ensure that the Maps app works most effectively, it has to be enabled in Location Services so that it can use your current location (**Settings** > **Privacy** > **Location Services** > **Maps** and select **While Using the App** under **Allow Location Access**).

When you tap in the Search box there are options for searching for nearby services, such as restaurants or transit stations. These are relevant to your current location.

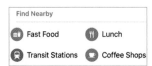

Looking Around Maps

With the Maps app you need never again wonder about where a location is, or worry about getting directions to somewhere. As long as you are connected to Wi-Fi or have a 5G/4G/3G network, you will be able to do the following: search maps around the world; find addresses, famous buildings or landmarks; get directions between different locations; and view traffic conditions.

Viewing your current location

To view your current location:

1. Tap once on the **Maps** app

2. Tap once on this button to view your current location

3. Double-tap on a map with one finger to zoom in (or swipe outward with thumb and forefinger)

4. Tap once with two fingers on a map to zoom out (or pinch inward with thumb and forefinger)

Finding locations

Within Maps you can search for addresses, locations, landmarks or businesses. To do this:

1. The Search box is at the top of the window

2. Enter an item into the Search box. As you type, suggestions appear underneath. Tap on one to go to that location

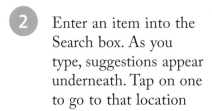

3 The location is shown on the map, in **Explore** view, and there is information about it in the left-hand panel

Satellite view

Locations can be viewed in great detail with Satellite view:

1 In Explore view, tap once on this button in the top right-hand corner

2 Tap once on the **Satellite** button

3 A satellite view of the location is displayed. Tap once on the **3D** button to view a graphics-rich 3D view of the location

You can also search for locations by postcode or zip code.

The graphics in 3D Satellite view have been updated in iPadOS 15.

Some locations provide a 3D Flyover tour. If this is available, a **Flyover** button will be displayed in Step 3.

163

Getting Directions

Finding your way around is an important element of using maps. This can be done with the Directions function:

1 Tap once in the Search box at the top of the window

2 Enter the destination and tap on one of the results (by default, the directions will be given from your current location)

3 Tap once on this button

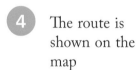

Hot tip

For some destinations alternative routes will be displayed, depending on distance and traffic conditions. Tap on the alternative route to select it, and tap on the **Go** button to proceed.

4 The route is shown on the map

5 Tap on each of these buttons at the bottom of the window to view the route for **Drive**, **Walk**, **Transit** or **Cycle**

6 Tap once on the **Go** button to start the directions and view step-by-step instructions on the map

7 The route is displayed, starting from your current location. Audio instructions tell you the directions to be followed. As you follow the route, the map and instructions are updated

To get back to the Start view, tap once on the **End Route** button from the box accessed in Step 8.

8 Swipe up from here to access the **Details** options for the route, which provides a step-by-step view of the route

Driving and Transit views

Two other map views can be used to view driving conditions and available transit options. To use these:

1 Tap once on the **Driving** button in Step 2 on page 163 to display a map with traffic conditions such as roadworks and traffic congestion

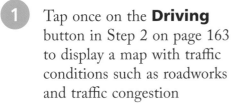

2 Tap once on the **Transit** button in Step 2 on page 163 to display a map with transit details such as trains, metros and ferries. Tap once on a transit item to view more details in the sidebar

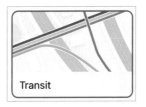

A number of cities have a selection of recommendations available within the Maps app. These are known as Guides and are available for cities including San Francisco, London, New York and Los Angeles. When you search for one of these cities, the Guide will be available in the results.

165

Traveling with your iPad

When you go traveling, there are a few essentials that you have to consider: passport, money and insurance, to name three. To this you can add your iPad: it is a perfect traveling companion that can help you plan your trip and keep you informed and entertained when you are away from home.

Uses for traveling

There are a lot of App Store apps that can be used for different aspects of traveling. However, the built-in apps can also be put to good use before and during your travels:

- **Notes**. Create lists of items to pack or landmarks that you want to visit.

- **Contacts**. Keep your Contacts app up-to-date so that you can use it to send postcards to friends and family. You can also use it to access phone numbers if you want to phone home.

- **Reminders**. Set reminders for important tasks such as changing foreign currency and buying tickets, and for details of flights.

- **Music**. Use this app to play your favorite music while you are traveling or relaxing at your destination.

- **Photos**. Store photos of your trip with this app and play them back as a slideshow when you get home.

- **FaceTime**. If you have a Wi-Fi connection at your destination you will be able to keep in touch using video calls.

- **Books**. Instead of dragging lots of heavy books around, use this app as your vacation library.

The **Clock** app can also be used to keep an eye on the time in different parts of the world; set alarms; and as a stopwatch and timer.

You can also use the **TV** app to download movies and TV shows. However, these will take up a significant amount of space on your iPad in terms of storage.

Planning your Trip

A lot of the fun and excitement of going on vacation and traveling is in the planning. The anticipation of researching new places to visit and explore can whet the appetite for what is ahead. The good news is, you can plan your whole itinerary while sitting in an armchair with your iPad on your lap. In the App Store there are apps for organizing your itinerary, and others for exploring the possibilities of where you can go:

TripIt

This is an app for keeping all of your travel details in one place. You have to register, which is free, and you can then enter your own itinerary details. Whenever you receive an email confirmation for a flight, hotel or car hire that you have booked, you can email this to your TripIt account and this will be added to your itinerary.

GetPacked

A great way to get peace of mind before you leave. This app generates a packing list and to-do lists to check before you leave, based on questions that you answer about your vacation and travel arrangements. You can then select items to include on your packing list, from clothes to documents and medical items.

Cool Escapes Maldives

For a little bit of luxury, try this app that enables you to search for hotels, restaurants and bars; view breathtaking photos; and get insider tips for this idyllic destination.

Although there is a small fee for the **GetPacked** app, it is well worth it, as it covers everything you will need to consider before you leave.

World atlas & world map

A comprehensive travel companion that offers a world atlas containing information about countries, cities, landmarks, airports and events. Navigate around the atlas with the same swiping and tapping gestures as the Maps app. Tap on an item to access a wealth of information about it.

Some map apps are free to download but then there is a fee to buy some of the associated maps.

Viewing Flights

Flying is a common part of modern travel, and although you do not have to book separate flights for a vacation (if it is part of a package) there are a number of apps for booking flights and also following the progress of those in the air:

Skyscanner

This app can be used to find flights at airports around the world. Enter your details such as the departure airport, destination and dates of travel. The results show a range of available options, covering different price ranges.

Flightradar24

If you like viewing the paths of flights that are in the air, or need to check if flights are going to be delayed, this app provides the real-time information you're looking for. Flights are shown according to flight number and airline.

Flight apps need to have an internet connection in order to show real-time flight information.

FlightAware Flight Tracker

Another app for tracking flights, showing arrivals and departures and also information about delays.

Finding Hotels

The internet is a perfect vehicle for finding good-value hotel rooms around the world. When hotels have spare capacity, this can quickly be relayed to associated websites, where users can usually benefit from cheap prices and special offers. There are plenty of apps that have details of thousands of hotels around the world, such as:

Tripadvisor

One of the top travel apps, this not only has hotel information but also restaurants, activities and flights. Enter a destination in the Search box and then navigate through the available options.

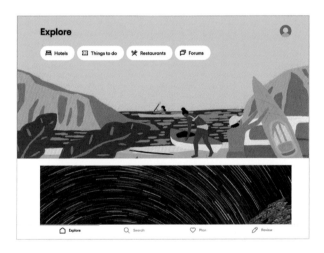

Hotels.com

A stylish app that enables you to enter search keywords for finding hotels based on destination, hotel name or nearby landmarks.

Booking.com Travel Deals

Another good, fully-featured hotel app that provides a comprehensive service and excellent prices.

lastminute.com

An app that specializes in getting the best prices by dealing with rooms that are available at short notice. Some genuine bargains can be found here, for hotels of all categories.

Hot tip

When booking flights and hotels, look up the price on your iPad, but check it on other, non-Apple, devices too; e.g. a Windows computer. Sometimes, different prices are displayed for searches from different types of devices.

Hot tip

Most hotel apps have reviews of all of the listed establishments. It is always worth reading these, as it gives you views from people who have actually been there.

Converting Currency

Money is always important in life, and never more so than when you are on vacation and possibly following a budget. It is therefore imperative to know the exchange rate of currencies in different countries compared with your own. Two apps that provide this service are:

XE Currency & Money Transfers

This app delivers information about exchange rates for all major world currencies and also a wealth of background information, such as high and low rates and historical charts.

Beware

When changing currency, either at home or abroad, always shop around to get the best rate. Using credit cards abroad usually attracts a supplementary charge too.

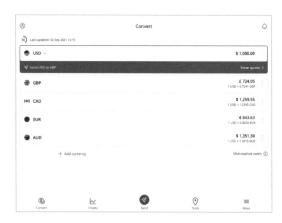

Currency

This app provides up-to-date exchange rates for over 150 currencies and 100 countries.

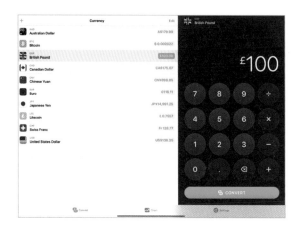

Travel Apps

Everyone has different priorities and preferences when they are on vacation. The following are some apps from the App Store that cover a range of activities and services:

- **Cities of the World Photo-Quiz**. An app to stimulate your wanderlust, with photo quizzes for recognizing over 110 famous cities. There are different types of quizzes, and also flashcards that provide the answers for you.

- **Disneyland Paris**. If you are entertaining your grandchildren at Disneyland Paris, this app will help you survive the experience. Maps, show times and descriptions of features help you organize all aspects of your visit.

- **Florida State Parks & Areas**. An extensive guide to the outdoor attractions of the Florida State Parks, including general information about all of the parks, advanced GPS maps and a built-in compass.

- **Google Earth**. Not just a travel aid, this app enables you to search the globe and look at photos and 3D maps of all your favorite places.

- **KAYAK**. A useful all-round app that compares hundreds of travel websites to get the best prices for flights, hotels and car rental. You can also create your own itineraries.

- **Language apps**. If you want to learn a new language for your travels, there is a wide range of apps to do this. These are located in either the Travel or Education categories in the App Store.

- **Magnifying Glass with Light**. Not just for traveling, this app acts as a torch and a magnifying glass all in one.

- **National Geographic Traveler**. Subscribe to this app to get an endless supply of high-quality travel features, photography and travel ideas.

- **New York Subway MTA Map**. Use this app to help you get around the Big Apple via the Subway. Plan your journeys and view live updates about stations and routes.

If you cannot find a certain app in the search results in the App Store, tap once on the **Filters** button, to the left of the Search box, and select the **Supports > iPhone Only** option. These apps can be downloaded for the iPad too, although they will have a smaller screen area to view the app.

There are several travel apps that have the functionality to mark locations that you have visited around the world. In the **Travel** section of the App Store, enter **places visited** (or similar) into the Search box, to view the matching apps.

...cont'd

The **Phrasebook** app comes with one free language. After that, you have to pay a small fee for each language that you want to use.

There are apps for displaying train times and details, but these are usually specific to your geographical location rather than covering a range of different countries.

- **Paris Travel Guide and Map**. A free map app for travel options around one of the great cities in the world.

- **Phrasebook**. Keep up with what the locals are saying in different countries with this app, which has useful phrases in over 30 languages.

- **Places Around Me**. Find a variety of different places near to your current location, wherever you are in the world. The app can be used to locate restaurants, hotels, banks, ATMs and a host of other useful establishments, relative to your current location.

- **Royal Caribbean International**. Find some of your favorite cruises with this app, which displays the full brochure of Royal Caribbean Cruises.

- **SIXT rent share and taxi**. Use this app for car rental, car sharing and taxis in over 100 countries.

- **Translate Free**. If you do not have the time or inclination to learn a new language, try this app to translate over 26 different languages.

- **Tube Map - London Underground**. Find your way around with this digital version of the iconic Tube Map. It includes live departure boards and station information.

- **Weather Live**. An app for showing the weather in locations around the world, with graphically-appealing forecasts, including extended forecasts for any coming day of the week or hour.

- **WiFi Connect**. It is always useful to be able to access Wi-Fi when you are on vacation, and sometimes essential. This app locates Wi-Fi hotspots in over two million locations worldwide.

- **Yelp: Local Food & Services**. Covering a range of information, this app locates restaurants, shops, services and places of interest in cities around the world.

11 Practical Matters

This chapter looks at some areas to enable you to have as much peace of mind as possible when using your iPad.

174 Finding your iPad

176 Avoiding Viruses

177 Privacy

178 Screen Time

181 Updating Software

182 Accessibility Issues

Finding your iPad

No one likes to think the worst, but if your iPad is lost or stolen, help is at hand. The Find My iPad function (operated through the iCloud service) allows you to send a message and an alert to a lost iPad, and also remotely lock it or even wipe its contents. This gives added peace of mind, knowing that even if your iPad is lost or stolen, its contents will not necessarily be compromised. To set up Find My iPad (before it becomes lost or stolen):

1 Tap once on the **Settings** app

2 Tap once on the **Apple ID, iCloud, Media & Purchases** account option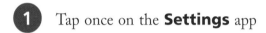

3 Tap once on the **Find My** option

4 Tap once on **Find My iPad** and drag the **Find My iPad** button **On** to be able to find your iPad on a map

Finding a lost iPad

Once you have set up Find My iPad you can search for it through the iCloud service, using another device. To do this:

1 Log in to your iCloud account at **www.icloud.com**

2 Click once on the **Find iPhone** button (this also works for the iPad)

3 Click once on the **All Devices** button and select your iPad. It is identified, and its current location is displayed on the map

Don't forget

Click once on the **Erase iPad** button in Step 5 to delete the iPad's contents. It is extremely important to have previously backed up your iPad content using iCloud (**Settings** > **Apple ID, iCloud, Media & Purchases** > **iCloud** > **iCloud Backup** > **On**) so that you can restore the content to a new device, or your original one if it is found.

4 Click once on the green circle to view details about when your iPad was located

5 Click once here to send a sound alert to your iPad. This can be useful if you have lost it in the house or close by

6 Click once here to lock your iPad

7 Enter a message that will appear on the iPad. Its existing 6-digit passcode will then be required to unlock it (if it does not have one, you will be prompted to add one)

Hot tip

If you are using Family Sharing (see pages 71-74) you can use the **Find My** app to locate the devices of other Family Sharing members.

Avoiding Viruses

As far as security from viruses on the iPad is concerned, there is good news and bad news:

- The good news is that, due to its architecture, most apps on the iPad do not communicate with each other so, even if there were a virus, it is unlikely that it would infect the whole iPad. Also, there are relatively few viruses being aimed at the iPad, particularly compared with those for Windows PCs.

- The bad news is that no computer system is immune from viruses and malware, and complacency is one of the biggest enemies of computer security. There have been some instances of photos in iCloud being accessed and hacked, but this was more to do with password security, or lack of, rather than viruses.

iPad security

Apple takes security on the iPad very seriously, and one way that this manifests itself is in the fact it is designed so that different apps do not talk to each other. This means that if there were a virus in an app, it would be hard for it to transfer to other apps and therefore spread across the iPad. Apple checks apps very rigorously, but even this is not foolproof, as shown in various attacks that have taken place against Apple devices.

Antivirus options

There are a few apps in the App Store that deal with antivirus issues, but do not actually remove viruses:

- **McAfee**. The online security firm has a number of apps that cover issues such as privacy of data and password security.

- **Norton**. Another popular online security option that has a range of apps to check for viruses and malware.

- **F-Secure SAFE**. Although not an antivirus app, this can be used to check websites that you are browsing, to alert you to suspicious sites and keep your details secure.

Don't forget

Malware is short for malicious software, designed to harm your computer, or access and distribute information from it.

176

Don't forget

Apple also checks apps that are provided through the App Store, and this process is very robust. This does not mean that it is impossible for a virus to infect the iPad, so keep an eye on the Apple website to see if there are any details about iPad viruses.

Privacy

The Privacy settings contain options for limiting how your apps use your location and also provide a report of app activity on your iPad. To use the Privacy settings:

1 Open the Settings app and tap once on the **Privacy** tab

2 Tap once on the **Location Services** option and turn it **On** to specify which apps can, and cannot, access your location. Tap once on the **Tracking** option to specify whether websites have to ask before they track your online activities

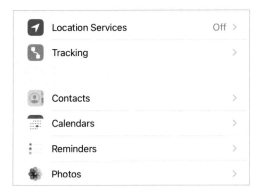

🧭	Location Services	Off >
🔗	Tracking	>
🖼	Contacts	>
📅	Calendars	>
⋮	Reminders	>
🌸	Photos	>

3 At the bottom of the Privacy window, tap once on the **Record App Activity** button

Record App Activity

4 Drag the **Record App Activity** button **On** to generate a weekly report about how the apps on your iPad access your data

‹ Privacy   **Record App Activity**

Record App Activity

Save a 7-day summary of when apps access your data, like your location or microphone, and see when apps or websites you visit within apps contact domains.

Save App Activity

Report information will be recorded as apps are used.

Recording App Activity is a new feature in iPadOS 15.

Screen Time

The amount of time that we spend on our digital devices is a growing issue in society, and steps are being taken to let us see exactly how much time we are spending looking at our mobile screens. In iPadOS 15, a range of screen-use options can be monitored with the Screen Time feature. To use this:

Once Screen Time has been turned On, it can be turned Off again by tapping once on the **Turn Off Screen Time** button at the bottom of the main Screen Time window.

If you select the **This is My Child's iPad** option in Step 4 you will be able to apply the same settings as for your own Screen Time options. In this instance, the child will need to have their own Apple ID.

Each week the Screen Time option produces a report based on the overall usage, as shown in Step 5. The report is identified with a notification when it is published each week.

1 Select **Settings** > **Screen Time**

2 Tap once on the **Turn On Screen Time** button

3 Options for using Screen Time are displayed. Tap once on the **Continue** button

4 Screen Time can be set up for your own use, or on a child's iPad. If it is set up for a child there will be more parental control options for controlling the type of content that is available. Tap once on an option

5 The current Screen Time usage is shown at the top of the panel at the right-hand side of the Settings window

Options for Screen Time

On the main Screen Time settings page there are options for viewing apps and content on your iPad:

1 Tap once on **Downtime**

Downtime
Off until schedule

2 Drag the **Downtime** button **On**, then turn the Scheduled button **On** and tap once on the **From** and **To** buttons to select times for when only specified apps are available

Don't forget

The time limit for using apps is only a suggestion, and the apps do not stop operating when the limit is reached. Instead, a notification appears to alert you to the fact that the time limit has been reached. Tap once on the **Ignore Limit** button to continue using the app.

3 Tap once on **App Limits**

App Limits
Set time limits for apps.

4 Tap once on the **Add Limit** button to add time limits for using types of apps

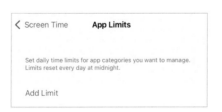

5 Select a category for the types of apps that you want to limit use of (or select **All Apps & Categories**). Tap once on the **Next** button to specify a time limit for how long these apps can be used

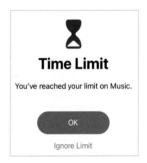

Time Limit
You've reached your limit on Music.

OK

Ignore Limit

Select an option for how long you want to ignore the time limit.

Ignore Limit For Today

Remind Me in 15 Minutes

One More Minute

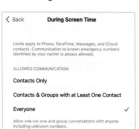

The options for allowing communications in Step 9 are: **Contacts Only**; **Contacts & Groups with at Least One Contact**; or **Everyone**.

...cont'd

6 Tap once on **Always Allowed**

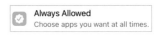

7 The apps that are always allowed to operate, regardless of what settings there are for Screen Time, are displayed. Tap once on the red circle next to one to remove it. Select items below the **Choose Apps** heading (further down the window) to add more

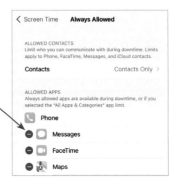

8 Tap once on **Communication Limits**

9 Tap once on **During Screen Time** or **During Downtime** to limit who can contact you, and communicate with you, during these times

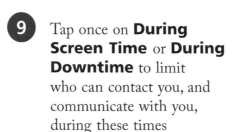

10 Tap once on **Content & Privacy Restrictions**

11 Drag the **Content & Privacy Restrictions** button **On** to apply restrictions for blocking inappropriate content

Updating Software

The operating system that powers the iPad is known as iPadOS. This is a mobile-computing operating system that is specifically tailored to the iPad. The latest version is iPadOS 15. Periodically, there are updates to iPadOS to fix bugs and add new features. These can be downloaded to your iPad once they are released:

If your iPadOS software is up-to-date, there is a message to this effect in the **Software Update** window.

1 Tap once on the **Settings** app

2 Tap on the **General** tab

3 Tap on the **Software Update** option

Software Update

4 If there is an update available (or a new version of iPadOS) it will be displayed here, with details of what is contained within it, from this link

Software Update can be set to be performed automatically overnight, when the iPad is charging and connected to Wi-Fi. To do this, tap on the **Automatic Updates** button in Step 4 and drag the **Download iPadOS Updates** button **On** to download the updates automatically. Drag the **Install iPadOS Updates** button **On** to have the updates installed automatically too.

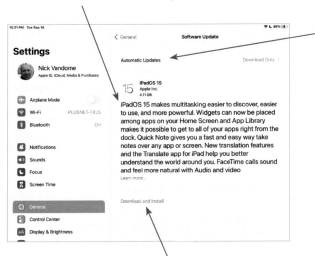

5 Tap once on the **Download and Install** link to start the download process. The iPadOS update will then download and install automatically

Accessibility Issues

The iPad tries to cater to as wide a range of users as possible, including those who have difficulty with vision or hearing, or those with physical and motor issues. There are a number of settings that can help with these areas. To access the range of accessibility settings:

1 Tap once on the **Settings** app

2 Tap on the **Accessibility** tab

3 The settings for **Vision**, **Physical and Motor**, **Hearing** and **General** are displayed here:

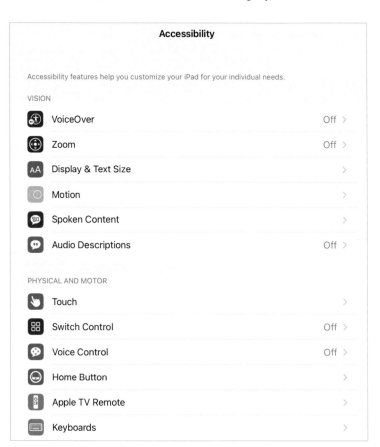

In the **Accessibility** > **Display & Text Size** section, drag the **On/Off Labels** button **On** to display an extra graphical symbol on the **On/Off** buttons, to further help identify their state.

Vision settings

These can help anyone with impaired vision, and there are options to hear items on the screen and also for making text easier to read:

1 Tap once on the **VoiceOver** option

2 Drag this button **On** to activate the VoiceOver function. This then enables items to be spoken when you tap on them

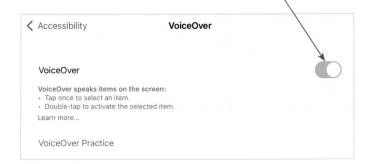

3 Select options for VoiceOver, as required

VoiceOver works with the built-in iPad apps and some apps from the App Store, but not all of them.

When VoiceOver is On, tap once on an item to select it and have it spoken; double-tap to activate the item.

There is a wide range of options for the way VoiceOver can be used. For full details, see the Apple website at **https://www.apple. com/accessibility/ vision/**

...cont'd

Don't forget

If you turn on the **Zoom** function, you can magnify areas of the screen with a magnification window. To activate this, double-tap with three fingers. Drag with three fingers within the window to view different areas of the screen, or press and hold on the tab in the middle bottom of the window to drag it into different positions.

Hot tip

Drag the **LED Flash for Alerts** button **On** in the Audio & Visual window to enable the screen to flash to indicate that an alert or a notification has been received.

4 Tap once on the **Accessibility** button to return to the main options

‹ Accessibility

5 Tap once on these options to access settings for zooming or magnifying the screen, and increasing the text size

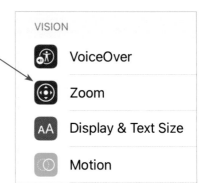

6 Tap again on the **Accessibility** button to return to the main options after each selection

Hearing settings

These can be used to change the iPad speaker from stereo to mono. To do this:

1 Tap once on the **Audio & Visual** button in the Hearing section and drag this button **On** to enable **Mono Audio**

2 Drag this button to specify whether sound comes out of the left or right speaker

AssistiveTouch

This can be used by anyone who has difficulty navigating around the iPad with the screen or buttons. It can be used with an external device such as a joystick, or it can be used on its own. To use AssistiveTouch (under **Physical and Motor > Touch**):

1 Tap once on the **AssistiveTouch** option

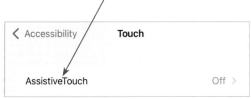

2 Drag this button **On** to activate the **AssistiveTouch** function

3 The AssistiveTouch icon appears on the screen and can be dragged around

4 Tap once on the AssistiveTouch icon to view its options

5 Tap once on the **Home** icon to return to the Home screen

The **AssistiveTouch** options make it easier for anyone with difficulties clicking the **Home** button, or using Multitasking Gestures.

The AssistiveTouch **Home** button option can be used if the physical **Home** button is ever damaged or does not work.

...cont'd

Tap on the **More** button in the **Device** window to select options for creating more gestures, shaking the iPad, capturing a screenshot and accessing the App Switcher window.

6 Tap on the **Device** icon in Step **4** on page 185

7 Tap once to activate the required function, including changing the screen rotation and adjusting the volume

Guided Access

The Guided Access option allows for certain functionality within an app to be disabled so that individual tasks can be focused on without any other distractions. To use this:

1 Under the **General** heading, tap once on the **Guided Access** option

2 Drag this button **On** to activate the Guided Access functionality

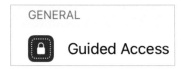

3 Open an app, and triple-click on the **Home** button to activate Guided Access within the app

4 Circle an area on the screen to disable it (this can be any functionality within the app). Tap on the **Start** button to activate Guided Access for that area. The circled area will not function within the app

A

Accented letters	84
Accessibility	182-186
AssistiveTouch	185-186
Guided Access	186
Hearing settings	184
Vision settings	183-184
Address book	138
AirDrop	38, 90
AirPod	39
AirPrint	139
Alarmed	140
Antivirus options	176
AnyList: Grocery Shopping List	140
Apple ID	103
Account recovery	103
Apple Music	144
Apple Pencil	10, 12
Deleting text	87
Instant Markup	12
Scribble	86
Selecting text	87
Writing	86-87
Apple Smart Keyboard	13, 76
Globe key	13
Shortcuts	13
Standard keyboard shortcuts	13
Apple TV	156
Apple TV+	156
Apple Watch	159
Apple Wireless Keyboard	76
App Library	36-37
Apps	8-9
Art	157
Built-in	91-93
Closing	51
Communication	116
Cookery	158
Deleting	100
Explained	90
Finding	95-97
Folders	99

Geographic availability	95
Health & Fitness	159
In-app purchases	97
Language	171
Organization	140
Organizing	99
Price	97
Travel	171-172
Apps (built-in)	
App Store	91
Books	91
Calendar	91
Camera	91
Clock	91
Contacts	91
FaceTime	91
Files	92
Find My	92
Home	92
iTunes Store	92
Mail	92
Maps	92
Measure	92
Messages	92
Music	92
News	92
Notes	93
Photo Booth	93
Photos	93
Podcasts	93
Reminders	93
Safari	93
Settings	91
Stocks	93
Tips	93
Translate	93
TV	93
Voice Memos	93
App Store	
About	94
Categories	95
Downloading apps	97
Finding apps	95-96
Searching for apps	96

Top Charts   96
    Updating apps   98
App Switcher   9, 13, 18, 50-53
Arcade   94
Art   157
AssistiveTouch   185-186

B

Background wallpaper or photos   17
Bamboo Paper   140
Battery power   11
Booking.com Travel Deals   169

C

Calendar and events   136-137
Cameras   11, 14, 146
Cellular settings   25
Charging.   See iPad: Charging
Cities of the World Photo-Quiz   171
Closing apps
    With App Switcher   51
Connectivity   11
Contacts   138
Control Center   38-41
Cooking   158
Cool Escapes Maldives   167
Currency   170

D

Dark Mode   24, 41
Dictation.   See Voice typing
Disneyland Paris   171
Dock   9, 28-29
Dolphin Web Browser   119
Do Not Disturb   58
Dragon Anywhere   88

Drawing   157
Dropbox   140

E

Email   104-105
    Setting up an account   104-105
    Viewing   105
Emojis.   See Messaging: Adding emojis
Evernote   140

F

Facebook   90, 116
FaceTime   110-114
    Creating links   113
    Microphone modes   112
    Receiving a call   112
    SharePlay   114
    Spatial sound   112
    Voice Isolation   112
Family Sharing   71-74
    Finding family members   74
    Setting up   71
    Sharing calendars   73
    Sharing music, books and movies 73-74
    Sharing photos   72
Find My app   74
Find My iPad   174-175
Fingerprint sensor with Touch ID   21
Firefox   119
Fitness   159
FlightAware Flight Tracker   168
Flightradar24   168
Florida State Parks & Areas   171
Flyover   163
Focus   58-61
Fraud warnings on websites   120
F-Secure SAFE   176
Full Window view.
        See Multitasking: Full Window view

G

Games	160
GetPacked	167
Getting online	102
Gmail	116
GoodReader PDF Editor & Viewer	140
Google Chrome	119
Google Earth	171

H

Handoff	28
Handwritten text	86
Health	159
Health app	159
Home button	9, 14, 18
HomePod	39
Home screen	17
Returning to	18, 26
Hotels.com	169

I

iA Writer	140
iCloud	66-69
Settings	67
iCloud+	68-69
iCloud Drive	70
iCloud Keychain	67
iMessages	106
In-app purchases. See Apps: In-app purchases	
Input/Output	11
Instagram	116
Instant Markup	12
Internet Service Provider (ISP)	102

iPad	10
Charging	22
Introduction	8
iPad Air	10
iPad mini	10
iPad Pro	10
Models	10
Simplicity	9
Wi-Fi and 5G/4G/3G connectivity	10
iPadOS 15	11, 16, 181
iPad Settings.	See Settings
iPhone	159
iTunes Store	142-143
Genius	143
Movies	143
Purchased	143
Top Charts	143
TV	143

K

KAYAK	171
Keeping notified	54-55
Keyboard	
Adding	76
Docking	78
Editing text	80
Entering text	79
Floating	78
Moving	78
Overview	76-77
Settings	82
Shortcuts	84-85
Slide typing	79
Splitting	78
Text abbreviations	85
Undocking	78
Keychain	67
Keynote app	140

L

Lastminute.com	169
Lightning Connector	14
Location Services	25
Locking your iPad	20
Lock screen	20-21
Showing notifications	20

M

Magnifying Glass with Light	171
Mail	105
Malware	176
Maps	162-165
Driving view	165
Explore view	163
Getting directions	164-165
Satellite view	163
Transit view	165
McAfee	176
Messages	106
Messaging	106-109
Adding emojis	108
Animated effects	108
Bubble effects	108
Screen effects	108
With iMessages	106-107
Mobile Security - Lookout	174
Multitasking	42-47
Buttons	42
Closing apps	44
Full Window view	47
Slide Over view	45-46
Split View	43-44
Multitasking Gestures	26-27
Moving between open apps	27
Moving between photos	27
Viewing notifications	27
Music	
Buying	142
Playing	144-145

N

National Geographic Traveler	171
News app	154-155
New York Subway MTA Map	171
Norton	176
Notability	140
Notes	128-133
Add Sketch	130
Creating notes	128
Formatting notes	128-129
Pinning notes	131
Quick Notes	132-133
Adding links	133
Notification Center	27, 55
Notifications	54-55
Numbers app	140

O

OfficeSuite	140
On/Off button	14
Opening items	19
Opera Browser	119
Operating system	11, 181

P

Pages app	140
Paris Travel Guide and Map	172
Passcode	
Adding	20
Photo Booth	151
Photos	146-151
Albums section	150
Composing with a grid	147
Copying	148
Editing	151
For You section	149
iCloud sharing	147